822.33 MAR
Marche, Stephen
How Shakespeare
everything

DATE

How
Shakespeare
Changed
Everything

ALSO BY STEPHEN MARCHE

Raymond and Hannah

Shining at the Bottom of the Sea

How
Shakespeare
Changed
Everything

Stephen Marche

HARPER

An Imprint of HarperCollins*Publishers*
www.harpercollins.com

B4T 5/11 21.99

Grateful acknowledgment for permission to reproduce illustrations
is made to the following: Aldridge Collection at the Charles Deering
McCormick Library of Special Collections, Northwestern University
Library: 8; Houghton Library, Harvard University: 10; Gregory
Crewdson: 75.

HarperCollins books may be purchased for educational, business, or
sales promotional use. For information, please write: Special Markets
Department, HarperCollins Publishers, 10 East 53rd Street,
New York, NY 10022.

FIRST EDITION

Designed by Ellen Cipriano

Library of Congress Cataloging-in-Publication Data

Marche, Stephen.
  How Shakespeare changed everything / by Stephen Marche.
    p.   cm.
Includes bibliographical references.
  ISBN 978-0-06-196553-1 (hardback)
1. Shakespeare, William, 1564–1616—Influence. I. Title.
PR2965.M27   2011
822.3'3—dc22

                                                      2010052856

11 12 13 14 15   OV/RRD   10 9 8 7 6 5 4 3 2 1

TO SARAH

CONTENTS

INTRODUCTION: ALL THE WORLD'S A STAGE

William Shakespeare was the most influential person who ever lived. He shaped our world more than any political or religious leader, more than any explorer or engineer. The gifted playwright who moves audiences to laughter and tears has also moved history. Do any other poets even begin to change our behavior or our environment? W. H. Auden once wrote that "poetry makes nothing happen. It exists in the valley of its saying where executives would never want to tamper." Shakespeare has wandered away from the valley of his saying and hangs around in the most unlikely places, in 1950s teen rebel movies and in psychoanalysts' offices, in nightclubs and in mall food courts, in voting booths in the American

ix

South and in the trash of Central Park. The effects of his words on the world have been out of all proportion, monstrous and sublime, vertiginous in their consequences, far beyond anything he could have predicted.

Shakespeare's power is evident everywhere if you know where to look. Shakespeare shows up in obvious places—he remains the dominant influence on Hollywood and Bollywood—but he also shows up in places you might never expect. The reason there are starlings in North America, the reason there are girls named Jessica, the reason there are skulls on teenagers' clothing—all Shakespeare. His appearances in American political life are surprising and profound. He was there when John Wilkes Booth shot Lincoln, and he was also there at the infancy of the civil rights movement. There would be no Obama if there were not first Othello, just as there would be no Leonardo DiCaprio if there were not first Romeo.

Shakespeare has changed your life, even if you've never read him or seen one of his plays. When I was a professor teaching Intro to Shakespeare, I started telling the stories in this book to impress upon students the vital importance of his plays to their lives. To people largely unfamiliar with his genius, the name Shakespeare can produce a vague impression of British stuffiness, of Cambridge dons in tweed and Wednesday matinees attended by school groups in rose gardens. The truth is that he belongs absolutely to our moment, to our experience. The world he created and inhabited is filthy and exalted, cheap and rarefied, gorgeous and vile, full of confusion and sudden epiphany; in short as full and complicated as our own. Nothing in literature captures the surging cacophony of voices and perspectives or the dazzling diversity of present-day cities such as London, New York, or Mumbai more than the plays of Shakespeare. He is more than ever our contemporary—a myriad-minded man for a myriad-minded world. When you become familiar with Shakespeare, you see him everywhere. The leaves change in the fall: "Bare ruined choirs where late the sweet birds sang." Madonna is in the news again: "Age cannot wither her, nor custom stale her infinite variety." Chilean miners are stuck half a mile underground: "The earth has bubbles as the water has." He is like a witty friend constantly making the perfect aside on whatever action the world is performing.

I came to Shakespeare almost by accident. In 2001, I was beginning my career as a novelist. There are two things an aspiring novelist needs: (1) As much free time as possible, and (2) a professional alibi so that when you attend a family reunion and your aunt asks you what you do, you have a respectable answer. I decided that doing a PhD would fulfill both requirements. But what would I study? I had to pick a subject to research intensely for five full years. I chose Shakespeare because I thought he would never bore me. And I was right. He has never bored me. My dissertation, which I completed at the University of Toronto in 2005, concerned various presentations of dead bodies in the 1540s and their effect on the drama fifty years later, a subject that was literally dry and dusty. But as I studied corpses, I became increasingly fascinated with (and distracted by) Shakespeare's weird influence on the living present. In this book, you will see how his influence extended into our bedrooms, into our mouths, into Hitler's Germany and Stalin's Russia and Churchill's England and the American Senate, and even into the sky. All that wonderful influence derives ultimately from his almost supernatural ability to move audiences. I learned when I was a professor that teaching Shakespeare to un- dergraduates is one of the easiest gigs in the history of the world. If you can't make a room full of young people care about Shakespeare, then you probably shouldn't be around young people or Shakespeare. He teaches himself. If a kid doesn't care about Hamlet or Macbeth or Othello, he or she is probably never going to care about any character in any book ever.

The breadth and depth of his appeal verges on the bizarre. I remember during one particularly dreary February in Toronto while I was studying for my PhD, locked in the library, I discovered the fascinating way in which the residents of Carriacou in the Grenadines take up Shakespeare. Every year, on Shrove Tuesday, young men, dressed in elaborate Pierrot-style costumes and animal masks topped with crowns of ficus roots, go from crossroads to crossroads, performing passages of *Julius Caesar* competitively. They call it the Shakespeare Mas. The game goes like this. One team captain shouts out a challenge to a member of the other team to recite a passage. (For example: "Will you relate to me Mark Antony's speech over Caesar's dead body?") If the competitor gets through the passage without error, he can ask his opponent to recite another passage. The contest is watched over by the huge crowds who scrutinize the speeches for mistakes. Players encourage their teammates with shouts of "brave," "tell him," "go on," and "that's right." Anyone who fails to recite the passage correctly or who mixes up the words earns a beating from his opponents. The whips used for these ceremonies are serious business, made from telephone wires. The government had to intervene in the 1950s when the Shakespeare Mas degenerated into a huge battle between the North and South island contingents, fueled by women who supplied the combatants with boiling water and stones. Everyone, throughout the proceedings, is hammered on the local overproof rum, Iron Jack.

When a folklore researcher asked one of the participants why they recited *Julius Caesar* and nothing else, his answer was simple, but there can be none better: Shakespeare was "sweeter." To illustrate his point, he burst into Mark Antony's famous speech: "O, pardon me, thou bleeding piece of earth."

Shakespeare's multitudinous effects on world history would have boggled his own capacious imagination. He's been the unwitting founder of intellectual movements he would never have endorsed and the secret presence behind spiritual practices he could never have imagined. He has been used as a crude political instrument by all sides in conflicts of which he could never have conceived. His vision has been assumed by saints and by murderers. At the bottom of all these slippery chains of consequences and perverted manifestations of his talent dwells the unique ability of Shakespeare to place his finger on people's souls. He has changed aspects of life as fundamental as the way we have sex, the words we use, how we classify youth and age. All that strange power, all his world-shaking, reality-transforming impact begins from a simple but mysterious truth: His stories sound good to everybody.

How

Shakespeare

Changed

Everything

THE FORTUNES
OF THE MOOR

"Othello has taken away from me all kinds of fears, all sense of limitation, and all racial prejudice," Paul Robeson told reporters in London after his opening night performance of the play in 1930. "Othello has made me free." How did Shakespeare become a champion of civil rights? How did he prepare the way for an African American president four hundred years after his death?

I used to teach Shakespeare in Harlem, at The City College of New York. I loved both the job and the neighborhood. Walking through Harlem is a bit like strolling through a run-down African American Florence, without the American tourists. There's the Apollo Theater, and nearby the house where Bessie Smith recorded her first vocals, there's the housing project where hip-hop was invented. I adored the students I was teaching, too. It's not every university where they attend class even when they're living out of their cars. The year before I was hired, City College had its first Rhodes Scholar in half a century, a Russian immigrant, and he had survived for a time by collecting bottles and spending his nights under the George Washington Bridge. My favorite student in my Graduate Seminar in Early Modern Tragedy lived with her mother and daughter in a single room in the West Bronx. She asked me for an extension for her term paper once. I asked for a reason. The father of her daughter was getting out of jail, she said, where he'd been in for murder, and since he had never seen his daughter, nobody knew how he was going to react. A little different from the "I'm a little depressed" or "I'm just so overloaded" I was accustomed to hearing at the University of Toronto. In a way it was the most flattering possible introduction to American life. I had thought this kind of American—the bootstrap American—was a myth, and yet there they were.

Maybe it was inevitable, given the surroundings, that while I was teaching in Harlem I also became convinced that Shakespeare was racist—so racist, I thought, that certain plays shouldn't be taught at the high school level. Since I had married a Jewish woman and we had a little Jewish son by then, I was already quite sure he was a rabid anti-Semite. There's no way that a play like *Othello* should be taught to kids, I came to believe.

But even as I was developing this conviction, I knew that Paul Robeson, the greatest Othello of the twentieth century and a lifelong champion of the African American struggle and human rights worldwide, would have screamed his opposition. Robeson found himself in Othello. And he found himself as an artist in Harlem. When he switched to Columbia Law School in 1921, he moved into an apartment across from the YWCA and began performing in occasional amateur theatricals. The Harlem Renaissance was peaking then, the neighborhood swelling with immigrants and fresh ideas, with the writings of W.E.B. Du Bois and Marcus Garvey, with black music from every part of the United States and the Caribbean and Africa. Robeson stumbled onto the lead in Eugene O'Neill's *The Emperor Jones*, the first serious play to explore black themes in New York's theater history, and later *All God's Chillun Got Wings*, the first dramatic exploration of interracial love. *Showboat* made him world-famous. Then *Othello*, which made him the most famous African American to that point in history. With its record-breaking Broadway run and extensive tour of the rest of the country, *Othello* became one of the primary expressions of black pride available in 1942, and Robeson's performances laid the groundwork for the civil rights movement twenty years later.

This, then, was the question I would ask my students at City College, who were surrounded on all sides by the evidence of African American suffering and triumph: How can a racist play become a vehicle for liberation?

Othello was a racist play in its original conception and incarnation. For sure. It relied for much of its effect on the inherent prejudice of an audience that feared Africans and Islam as a commonplace, an audience for whom a Moor was inherently a barbarian whose very flesh was abject and terrifying. In the play's opening scene, as Iago whips the city of Venice into a fury over Othello's elopement with Desdemona, Shakespeare keeps hammering home the town's disgust with mixed-race sex: "an old black ram is tupping your white ewe"; "you'll have your daughter covered with a Barbary horse"; "making the beast with

4

two backs" and "the gross clasps of a lascivious Moor" all deploy within the space of fifty lines. Othello's first words ("'Tis better as it is") belie his persecutors' hysteria, but the calm dignity of his bearing is always intended to contrast with the brutality of his body. Just as Macbeth is a good man whose inherent ambition undoes him, and just as Lear is a good king whose inherent pride breaks him, Othello is a man whose inherent barbarism undoes his civilization. The action of the play is a long stripping away of his superficial accomplishment to reveal the burnished inner truth. The inner truth of Othello is the unavoidable savagery of his blackness.

For most of its history, the problem with *Othello* was that it wasn't racist enough. Three of the greatest Shakespeare critics of all time singled out the love between Othello and Desdemona for their disapproval. Charles Lamb found "something extremely revolting in the courtship and wedded caresses of Othello and Desdemona." Samuel Taylor Coleridge thought the idea that a white woman could fall in love with an African was beyond the realm of the believable: "It would be something monstrous to conceive this beautiful Venetian girl falling in love with a veritable Negro." "To imagine is one thing," commented the scholar A. C. Bradley, "and to see is another."

The outrage of these critics—and let's not hide from the fact that they were some of the most intelligent men of their respective times and places—was stirred by what Bradley, with characteristic self-consciousness and brilliance of phrase, describes as "an aversion of the blood" to the bedroom scene in the fifth act. A black man murdering his wife in the marital bed. It is a testament to the power of racial abjection, to the raw physicality of the hatred of black flesh, that the setting of a black man with a white woman in a bedroom is the ideal scene for the most horrific murder in any of Shakespeare's tragedies. The representation of the married mixed-race couple in their nuptial bed has been, for many audiences in many countries, more subversively horrifying than the murder itself. Othello is perpetually being interrupted in private moments with his wife. He is roused from his marital bed at the play's beginning, and again in Cyprus in the second act. Samuel Johnson found the scene "not to be endured." But the various critical reactions do little more than proceed from where the horrified Venetian spectators onstage begin. Lodovico sums up their reaction perfectly: "The object poisons sight: Let it be hid."

In the nineteenth century, actors and directors solved the problem of Othello's offensive blackness by interpreting "Moor" as "Arab," and toning down his skin color. Thus the "bronze age" of Othello. Only one African American actor, Ira Aldridge, managed to make a go of it in the 1830s. Several British critics of the day believed him to be entirely the equal of the great Charles Kean, and he was so relevant an interpreter of Shakespeare that he even performed other characters in whiteface—his Macbeth was an enormous success in Russia. (Shylock was his most famous role other than Othello.)

He was widely praised when he was touring the provinces, and was one of the most influential Shakespearean actors in Continental Europe. He, too, like Robeson, slept with white women in real life as well as in character (his second wife was Swedish) and used his prominence to advocate for his people. After one performance where the ovations demanded a speech, an eyewitness recorded his dignified statement: "He hoped the prejudice was

In the 1830s, Ira Aldridge
triumphed in whiteface as
Shylock and Lear.

fast dying away, when one man should be deprived of a hearing on the stage, because his face was of another colour, seeing the black man and the white were both the work of the same Creator." Even before the abolition of slavery, his powers as an actor allowed Aldridge a venue to state his case for his common humanity.

All the success in the provinces could not earn Aldridge praise in the places that mattered most, London and New York. Aldridge appeared for two performances of *Othello* at Covent Garden in 1833. The *Figaro* was outraged: "A further act of insolence is to be perpetrated, by the introduction to the boards of Covent Garden theater, of that miserable nigger, whom we found in the provinces imposing on the public by the name of the *African Roscius*." In New York, the idea of an African American performer on any stage at all was an impossibility. In place of *Othello*, the most popular dramatic show of the time was the minstrel skit "Jim Crow." Thomas "Daddy" Rice, the actor who originated that character, also invented a minstrel burlesque *Otello* in 1847, a parody of "the noblest nigger of dem all!"

Othello was a popular play in the antebellum South, although the lead grew paler and paler with the approach

The playbill from the National Theatre in Cincinnati, 1847.

of the Civil War. By the 1850s, Othello was made to fit into the novelistic convention of the "sad octoroon," played with light makeup and few black features. Actors chose the lightest bronze skin tone possible, because they were terrified of the reaction a black face—even a Caucasian face slightly smeared with burnt champagne cork—might provoke from Southern audiences.

When Paul Robeson arrived in the early twentieth century with his strong black features, his physical presence alone was an attack on the humiliated, blanched Othello. His first chance at the part came in London in the thirties, when he was touring with *Showboat*. The contradictions of being an African American celebrity were not quite as pronounced in England as they were in the States but proved confounding nonetheless. As he toured the British coasts giving concerts, he was regularly received by huge greeting committees; he was given the keys to various cities; cabdrivers refused payment. And yet the Savoy Grill might decide, as it did when he arrived as the guest of Lady Colefax, that it didn't serve Negroes. Despite his misgivings about his own abilities, when a London theater producer named Maurice Browne offered him $15,000 a week to play the Moor, he couldn't refuse. The part and the money were just too good, although the stakes could not have been higher. While in rehearsal, Robeson and the director received several letters objecting to the sight of a black man kissing a white woman, and that particular objection, more than any other, upset and terrified Robeson, made him feel, as he said, like "a plantation hand in the parlor—that clumsy."

The London version of *Othello* starring Robeson featured bungled direction, terrible lighting, and stupid costumes, and worse, did not provide its star with the training he begged for. Still he received a standing ovation on opening night and positive reviews in the daily papers. The weeklies were colder. The discrepancy between these responses might seem odd but makes sense given the social context of the performance. The audiences were overwhelmed by the political act they were witnessing; only later did the quality of the artistic act come to mind. Robeson was the first to admit that he wasn't a very good Othello. He was too modest to admit the equally plain truth that he was a great Othello.

History overtook Shakespeare in a uniquely fortuitous way. Hindsight tends to make us see our ancestors as more racist and prejudiced than they saw themselves.

#141 08-05-2019 11:33AM
Item(s) checked out to p24812201.

TITLE: How Shakespeare changed everythin
BARCODE: 1060004943310
DUE DATE: 08-26-19

TITLE: A dog's way home
BARCODE: 1060006377560
DUE DATE: 08-26-19

TITLE: Ultimate Spider Man ultimate co
BARCODE: 10600065
DUE DATE: 08-26-19

TITLE: Complete works
BARCODE: 1060003896004
DUE DATE: 08-26-19

TITLE: William Shakespeare's A midsummer
BARCODE: 1060001736624
DUE DATE: 08-26-19

Avon Library 949-6797
To renew items, please go to evld.org.

Your grandmother uses the word *negro* and you squirm; to her it's just a descriptor. Shakespeare is the opposite. As time progresses, he seems more open-minded than he would have been considered in his own time. Sometimes it's better that we don't understand the consequences of our actions. We can do good despite our corrupt motives.

Shakespeare's humanism saved him. His plays may be full of stereotypes—of Moors, of Welshmen, of the French—but he never loses his sense of shared humanity. Integrating his time's contempt for the Muslim African Other in his portrayal of Othello, he also reveled in the glorious individuality of the character. Othello's Christian and Moorish sides clash in a burst of self-destruction, encapsulated perfectly by his suicide, which he himself describes in his final speech as a struggle between his two natures.

> Soft you; a word or two before you go.
> I have done the state some service, and they
>   know't.
> No more of that. I pray you, in your letters,
> When you shall these unlucky deeds relate,
> Speak of me as I am; nothing extenuate,

Nor set down aught in malice: then must you
　　speak
Of one that loved not wisely but too well;
Of one not easily jealous, but being wrought
Perplex'd in the extreme; of one whose hand,
Like the base Indian, threw a pearl away
Richer than all his tribe; of one whose subdued
　　eyes,
Albeit unused to the melting mood,
Drop tears as fast as the Arabian trees
Their medicinal gum. Set you down this;
And say besides, that in Aleppo once,
Where a malignant and a turban'd Turk
Beat a Venetian and traduced the state,
I took by the throat the circumcised dog,
And smote him—thus!

> *He stabs himself*
> (5.2.336–354)

Othello's Christian side destroys his pagan side, and vice versa; his civilization—his choice of Desdemona—can only cover, it cannot change his primitive blackness. But his dignity as well as his primitiveness is inescapable.

The brand of racism prevalent in American culture in the 1930s and 1940s (and beyond) reduced African American actors and singers to figures of comedy and humiliation. I own a small book called *Phunology* from 1923—a collection of fun games and activities for social occasions. One of the suggestions for Halloween reads as follows:

Spook Minstrels.—A clever spook minstrel could be worked out. Two spooks capture a negro who, on being asked his name, answers "Sambo," and on a further demand for his other name tremblingly informs his captors that his "maiden name am Johnson." Mephisto and a ghost chorus now enter the scene of action, and one of the ghosts informs the negro that he need not fear, for it's no one but "Mephistopheles." "Mephiswhoforlee?" queries Sambo. "Mephisto, Mephistopheles." "Well," answers Sambo, "it looks like the devil to me."

The spooks then threaten to skin the minstrel and roast him like a pig, during which scene the authors suggest that "wieners and rye bread or ginger snaps and sweet cider" be served. The character of Othello is the perfect rebuttal of this sick little joke. Othello has seen the devil. He's seen Iago, the one who is not who he is. Othello's eloquence is the definition of gentlemanliness: martial, plainspoken, decisive. The role commands respect. In the black place which the American consciousness has reserved for illiteracy and trembling, *Othello* insists on dignity and nobility. The meaning of his death radiates to encompass all of us. The fragility of civilization may have been an idea that Shakespeare saw as peculiarly relevant to a Moor living in Venice, but it is equally relevant to everyone here and now. We all have a barbarism we are trying to clamp down.

In 1930, Robeson was not ready to be Othello but tried anyway. By 1942 he was ready. As his costar Uta Hagen recalled later, "He had judgment about himself that was astonishing. He didn't fall for praise—other people's accolades never went to his head." In 1930, he and the director, Margaret Webster, had relied on his huge athleticism and booming voice for the effects; nobody had wanted him to act. In 1942, he insisted on putting together a real performance. The effect was the most popular Broadway Shakespeare of all time. The first night he gave the role (at a university out of town in order to gauge America's willingness for him in the role), he redefined *Othello* forever. The *New York Times* declared: "A Negro actor is acceptable, both academically and practically." *Variety* believed that, after Robeson, "no white should ever dare presume" to play Othello again. When the show opened on Broadway, on October 19, 1942, the night ended with a twenty-minute ovation, and even when Uta Hagen gave a grateful speech, the audience wouldn't relent. Robeson gave 296 continuous performances of *Othello* on Broadway, smashing the previous record for a Shakespeare play, which was 157. The power of the play was in direct relation to the power of the taboo it was violating. Fascinated Americans turned up in droves to watch the spectacle of a dignified black man and his love for a pale white woman.

Robeson immediately turned his fame to the service of politics. He addressed the owners of major league baseball on the subject of desegregating the sport, the first time they had listened to an African American making a plea on the subject. He performed a scene from the play at a fund-raiser for a communist city council candidate named Ben Davis, who went on to win his seat.

The play was a vehicle for other kinds of liberation as well. As the production began to tour Canada and the United States, the situation offstage began to grow nearly as complicated as the one onstage. Robeson's costars were Joe Ferrer as Iago and his wife, Uta Hagen, as Desdemona. One night while Robeson and Hagen were waiting in the wings, according to Hagen's memoirs: "He took his *enormous* hand—costume and all—and put it between my legs. I thought, What *happened* to me?! I was being assaulted in the most phenomenal way, and I thought, What the hell, and I got unbelievably excited. I was flying!" Her husband was already having an affair with somebody else in the cast and so was quite happy to pass off his wife—a perfectly Iagoish move—although they all returned to their original beds whenever they returned to New York. According to Hagen, when she became pregnant, Robeson hit her in a drunken rage, which she believed contributed to her miscarriage. Shakespeare held the mirror up to nature, but the cast did a good job of reflecting *Othello* as much as possible in their daily lives. They brought *Othello* to America onstage and off.

And everywhere they went on the tour they were

always in America. At the Café Society in Greenwich Village, a white Southerner shouted that his surname was also Robeson, so his father had probably owned Paul Robeson's father. "You probably belong to me," he shouted. A hotel in Indianapolis fitted a back office with a cot for Robeson's reservation. Told that the room was unacceptable, the clerk replied, smiling: "Then Mr. Robeson will not be staying here?" In Boston, Robeson and Hagen were coming down in an elevator, with their arms linked. The door opened. A woman entered, saw them, and spat in Uta Hagen's face.

As Robeson toured *Othello*, he was bringing the idea of a dignified black man and the possibility of interracial love to the widest audience he could reach. He was doing it onstage every night and offstage every day. How effective was Robeson? So effective that in 1950, he received the ultimate compliment from officials of the United States government. They revoked his passport. His earnings fell from over $100,000 a year to just $6,000.

Between Shakespeare and us lies the historical chasm of what Walt Whitman described as "the foulest crime in history known in any land or age." Shakespeare could not have imagined Paul Robeson kissing Peggy Ashcroft onstage, but neither could he have imagined the three hundred years of the dehumanization of black flesh that separated him from Robeson. Slavery makes miscegenation the ultimate crime, because the act demonstrates the basic biological truth that whites and blacks are the same species, and the recognition of common humanity, in an economic system based on the denial of that humanity, is utterly subversive.

Robeson, through sheer will, forced Shakespeare to serve the truth. So has Obama. Throughout the 2008 election, he retold *Othello* obliquely and redemptively. He appeared exactly as Othello does at the beginning of the play: a man who has overcome a difficult past through personal merit; an outsider, courageous, supremely eloquent, capable of resolving factional struggle through sheer force of charisma. That's the 2008 election in a Hollywood pitch: Othello with a black wife. The campaign offered the world a chance to begin *Othello* again, to start over where the powerful Moor, perfect in virtue and a paragon of nobility, arrives to lead the Republic through its time of crisis. Part of Obama's genius was the ability to deflect and control the *Othello* narrative, which is irreducibly present in the public consciousness. People do not understand stories they haven't heard before. The fact that 18 percent of Americans still believe that Obama is a Muslim, the continuing power of the birther movement despite the clear-cut evidence that he was born in America, testify to *Othello*'s power as a prepared narrative. For many Americans, Obama remains a noble Moor in the mold that Shakespeare cast.

Back to my students in Harlem, where Robeson began: What was Shakespeare's contribution to their surroundings? It was amazing how little any of my questions about race mattered to them. I would bring up the history and no one would want to talk about it. Not that they weren't interested in the plays. It's just that my students had other concerns. What about the gay subtext between Othello and Cassio? Was Desdemona's passivity partly to blame for the tragedy? The handkerchief was far more interesting to my students than the color of Othello's skin.

"Othello has made me free," Paul Robeson said. But from what? The ground keeps falling out from under us. Only Shakespeare keeps landing on his feet.

WORDS,
WORDS, WORDS

A fact to make you feel instantly more cultured and smarter: Already, without trying, you quote Shakespeare all the time.

> A *jaded fortune-teller panders* to her *widowed employer*.
> A *bloodstained bandit cows* a *domineering mountaineer*.
> An *advertising manager* adds *excitement* to *skim milk*.

You can legitimately claim that you sprinkle your speech with Shakespearean terms: *Abstemious, academe, accused*, *addiction*, *alligator*, *amazement*, *anchovy*, *arouse*, *assassination*, *auspicious*. They're all his invention. And those are just the obvious ones from the *A*s.

The exact number of words Shakespeare added to the English language can't be known. Word origins in general are notoriously difficult to determine. We know that Gelett Burgess invented the word *blurb* at a New York dinner party in 1907, but for the most part, English terms emerge tentatively, out of a miasma of hints and feints and half sense. Besides, there's no way to tell whether Shakespeare plucked a word out of his head or off the street. Most scholars agree that he coined somewhere in the vicinity of seventeen hundred words—far more than any other writer in any language. It's an even more astonishing feat when you consider that nearly 10 percent of Shakespeare's vocabulary of twenty thousand terms was new to him and to his audience. In a sense, he's easier to understand now, because we are familiar with words like *farmhouse* and *eyeball* and *softhearted* and *watchdog*. We've lost an entire dimension of the original Shakespeare experience. Imagine going to a new play and hearing for the first time *sanctimonious* or *lackluster* or *fashionable*. That freshness is lost to our ears.

Some of his best words are fancy, big Latinate words like *consanguineous*. He built many such words by fusing prefixes and suffixes onto preexisting words. *Con-* means "with." *Sanguine* means "blood." Therefore *consanguineous* means "of the same blood" or "related by blood." Other words are foreign borrowings that he anglicized, such as the word *bandit* from the Italian *banditto*. Others, such as *hint* or *hush*, come from resuscitated Middle English words. He nouned verbs and verbed nouns. That's how we have *to dawn* and *to elbow* out of the way. He made adjectives like *deafening*. He made adverbs like *tightly*. He made crazy words like *buzzer* and *kickshaw* and *zany*. Shakespeare is the special-effects master of everyday speech. He is, as Virginia Woolf put it, "the word-coining genius, as if thought plunged into a sea of words and came up dripping."

To me, his facility with linguistic manipulation— mixing and matching and fusing terms—is less impressive than his preternatural ability to match the sound of a word to its sense. I mean, it's one thing to make up a word like *metamorphize*. That just requires brilliance and education and open-mindedness. But *glow*? Or *gnarled*? Or *hobnob*? Or *gossip*? That's *al di la*, as Connie Francis sings it—beyond the beyond. Once he finds the form of a word, it stays that way forever. The perfection of his invented words, rather than their quantity, is awe inspiring. He invented *traditional* and *eventful*. How did people live without them?

The name Jessica from *The Merchant of Venice* may be his single greatest accomplishment. Nobody uses the name just because Shakespeare made it up. For four hundred years, parents have been naming their daughters Jessica because they love the sound of it. That's truly astonishing. His expressions have an amazing lasting power. The British journalist Bernard Levin once produced a handy list of them:

> If you cannot understand my argument, and declare "It's Greek to me," you are quoting Shakespeare; if you claim to be more sinned against than sinning, you are quoting Shakespeare; if you recall your salad days, you are quoting Shakespeare; if you act more in sorrow than in anger, if your wish is father to the thought, if your lost property has vanished into thin air, you are quoting Shakespeare; if you have ever refused to budge an inch or suffered from green-eyed jealousy, if

you have played fast and loose, if you have been tongue-tied, a tower of strength, hoodwinked or in a pickle, if you have knitted your brows, made a virtue of necessity, insisted on fair play, slept not one wink, stood on ceremony, danced attendance (on your lord and master), laughed yourself into stitches, had short shrift, cold comfort or too much of a good thing, if you have seen better days or lived in a fool's paradise—why, be that as it may, the more fool you, for it is a foregone conclusion that you are (as good luck would have it) quoting Shakespeare; if you think it is early days and clear out bag and baggage, if you think it is high time and that that is the long and short of it, if you believe that the game is up and that truth will out even if it involves your own flesh and blood, if you lie low till the crack of doom because you suspect foul play, if you have your teeth set on edge (at one fell swoop) without rhyme or reason, then—to give the devil his due—if the truth were known (for surely you have a tongue in your head) you are quoting Shakespeare; even if you bid me good riddance and send me packing, if you wish I was dead as a doornail, if you think I am an eyesore, a laughing stock, the devil incarnate, a stony-hearted villain, bloody-minded or a blinking idiot, then—by Jove! O Lord! Tut, tut! For goodness' sake! What the dickens! But me no buts—it is all one to me, for you are quoting Shakespeare.

He invented so many expressions that have entered daily life that it's nearly impossible not to notice them when attending a production of the plays. Especially when the actors don't have the rhythm of the poetry down, the well-known phrases stick out like neon Coke ads on the side of a dour Tudor castle. To theater people, the quality of a Shakespeare performance depends on the originality of the direction, the profundity of the interpretation, the effectiveness of the sets, and so on. In my experience, there are two kinds of Shakespeare performances for most audiences: (1) They can understand the words, (2) they can't understand the words. They like 1 and they don't like 2. Margaret Webster, the great director of the thirties and forties, in her memoir *Shakespeare Without Tears*, recalled an actor (whose name she mercifully forgot) reciting in place of his lines:

The Earl of Whatsisname, Lord Something Else
Some kind of Bishop and two other guys
Capitulate against us, and are up.

Nobody except the director noticed.

Shakespeare is full of "greatest hits" moments, bits memorized at school, lines quoted often in the press, and passages so famous it is impossible to hear them without being distracted from the dramatic matter at hand. The moment every actor dreads in *Hamlet* is beginning the first soliloquy of act three. A rustle of recognition rises from the crowd. Everybody already knows the speech. A few of them even know when the actor screws up.

To be, or not to be—that is the question:
Whether 'tis nobler in the mind to suffer
The slings and arrows of outrageous fortune,
Or to take arms against a sea of troubles,
And by opposing end them. To die, to sleep—
No more; and by a sleep to say we end
The heart-ache and the thousand natural shocks
That flesh is heir to—'tis a consummation
Devoutly to be wished: to die, to sleep.

To sleep, perchance to dream. Ay, there's the rub;
For in that sleep of death what dreams may come,
When we have shuffled off this mortal coil,
Must give us pause. There's the respect
That makes calamity of so long life.

(3.1.55–68)

It is impossible to hear the speech now without hearing the schoolmaster reciting it. Even though the subject is suicide, and how fear obscures our consciousness of life's pointlessness, the well-fed audiences nod along to the well-known music of the verse. It just sounds so Shakespearey.

No famous Shakespeare passage works better for parody than "To be, or not to be." During the nineteenth century, comic, rhyming burlesques of Shakespeare's serious plays became a mania. And "To be, or not to be" was a rich seam to be mined for ridicule. In *Hamlet! The Ravin' Prince of Denmark!!* (1816), the prince recites the speech after eating too much:

> *"To be or not to be, that is the question,"*
> *Oh dear! I'm suffering from the indigestion!*

"Whether 'tis nobler in the mind to suffer
The slings and arrows of "—a paltry duffer;
"Or to take arms, and by opposing end them"—
These rhymes are very poor, I can't amend them—
To sleep away the pain of too much grub;
"To sleep—perchance to dream—aye there's the
 rub."
Than this no "consummation" could be betterer,
"For who would bear the whips and scorns," et
 cetera—
I really can't go on, for people say
This is the noblest passage of the play!

In 1813, *Hamlet Travestie* converted the speech into a song, to the tune of "Here we go up, up, up," which I hope was funnier in performance than it is on the page.

When a man becomes tir'd of his life,
The question is, "to be, or not to be?"
For before he dare finish the strife,
His reflections most serious ought to be.

(It goes on for eight verses.)

The fashion for burlesque disappeared with the nineteenth century, although more recently Prince Charles, who often seems as though he still lives in the nineteenth century, made a pretty decent attempt to turn the speech into modern English:

> Well, frankly, the problem as I see it at this moment in time is whether I should just lie down under all this hassle and let them walk all over me, or whether I should just say OK, I get the message, and do myself in. I mean, let's face it, I'm in a no-win situation, and quite honestly, I'm so stuffed up to here with the whole stupid mess that I can tell you I've just got a good mind to take the easy way out. That's the bottom line. The only problem is, what happens if I find, when I've bumped myself off, there's some kind of . . . ah, you know, all that mystical stuff about when you die, you might find you're still—know what I mean?

Unfortunately parodies of Shakespeare are not always intentional. The minor industry of mugs and magnets offers pearls of Shakespearean wisdom extracted from context and often misquoted. They drive me insane. I recall a pub in Stratford, Ontario, whose menu featured a line from *Henry IV, Part II*: "Doth it not show vilely in me to desire a small beer?" (The idea being to force you away from the half pint for lunch.) The line should read "Doth it not show vilely in me to desire small beer?" Prince Hal is wondering why he wants thin beer—that's what "small beer" means—when he's a prince who could afford to drink anything he likes. The much-T-shirted line from *Henry VI*, "the first thing we do, let's kill all the lawyers," comes from a wisecracking scumbag named Dick the Butcher. In context, the line is a testament to why we need lawyers.

Shakespeare tends to put his "wisest" expressions in the mouths of blithering idiots and the nastiest villains. A preacher might well quote:

> Good name in man and woman, dear my lord,
> Is the immediate jewel of their souls.
> Who steals my purse steals trash; 'tis something-
>   nothing;
> 'Twas mine, 'tis his, and has been slave to
>   thousands:

33

But he that filches from me my good name
Robs me of that which not enriches him
And makes me poor indeed.

(3.3.158–164)

The preacher would tell you it's Shakespeare. The preacher might even mention that the lines come from *Othello*. But for the lines to have the desired effect, he would have to forget that their speaker is Iago, the ultimate villain, the motiveless malignity. Most of the wisdom in *Hamlet*—"neither a borrower nor a lender be," "the apparel oft proclaims the man," "to thine own self be true"—comes from a single litany given by Polonius, a man who shows no signs of intelligence at any other point in the play.

Henry Crawford in Jane Austen's *Mansfield Park* declared that "Shakespeare one gets acquainted to without knowing how . . . His thoughts and beauties are so spread abroad that one touches them every where, one is intimate with him by instinct." He's right. Shakespeare invented "snail-paced" and "green-eyed" and "crack of doom" and "fool's paradise." He invented the expression "the be-all and the end-all." Nobody since has found a better way to

34

express the thought of finality. More even than so many wonderful words and expressions, his greatest gift was the spirit he bequeathed to the English language, a spirit of expressive appropriation rather than economical clarity. English speakers think nothing of stealing words and phrases wherever we find them—*boondocks* is a great English word; it also comes from Tagalog. We talk about a man who possesses a certain je ne sais quoi without worrying about whether mixing English with French is treason. Shakespeare made language theft acceptable in English.

The result has been the largest vocabulary of any language on earth. I adore the sheer number of our words. Every time I write, I feel I'm sitting down at an old, beautiful, immense organ with infinite modes and registers and effects. It is truly a magnificent inheritance. I once had a conversation with the Israeli short story writer Etgar Keret about writing in modern Hebrew versus writing in English. His language is ancient but also brand-new, forcing him to invent words all the time. When we spoke he had just published a collection—later translated as *The Nimrod Flip-Out*—in which he had had to come up with a Hebrew word that meant "crazy in a good way." Such inventions are never necessary in English (although they can be fun to do anyway). There always already exists a term that captures the precise shade of any desired connotation. In Hebrew there is one word for *prostitute*, the word from Genesis, *zanah*. In English there's *prostitute*, *whore*, *harlot*, *trollop*, *escort*, *hooker*, *strumpet*, *courtesan*, *streetwalker*, and *call girl*. And that's before slang expressions such as "woman of easy virtue" or "lady of the night" or the other various bits of nastiness. English has a distinct word for every historical period and price point and motivation. Hebrew has *zanah*.

Shakespeare's impact on our speech is easily the greatest sign of his power. He has changed the horizons of thought for billions through his words. And yet maybe no writer had less faith in words than Shakespeare. His work is full of words that fail, meanings that fall apart, ironies that nobody understands. Polonius asks what Hamlet is reading and he replies, "words, words, words." When Caesar's deceptive emissary leaves Cleopatra, she says, "he words me, girls, he words me." It sounds like a despicable and humiliating sexual act.

My favorite Shakespearean words are *prenzie* and *scamels*. Know what they mean? If so, write me, because nobody else does. *Prenzie* comes from *Measure for Mea-*

sure. Several editors have suggested that the word is a typographical error for *princely*. I find it hard to reduce the matter to a typo: The word *princely* is printed correctly five times in *Measure for Measure*, and *prenzie* is used twice, first to describe "the prenzie Angelo" and second time to describe his clothes. "Upright" has recently been suggested, but I don't buy it. It just doesn't make sense with the clothes. Upright clothes? So *prenzie* must mean something—we just don't know what.

Caliban from *The Tempest* gives us the other great Shakespearean word we don't understand:

> And I with my long nails will dig thee pig-nuts;
> Show thee a jay's nest, and instruct thee how
> To snare the nimble marmoset; I'll bring thee
> To clustering filberts, and sometimes I'll get thee
> Young scamels from the rocks.
>
> (2.2.165–169)

Nobody knows what a scamel is. It could be a typo for *sea-mew*, another term for gull. Or it could be a word that just Caliban knows—a gift from Shakespeare after denying the monster his own language.

We should feel free to make up new meanings for these words. *Prenzie*, I think, should mean *princely* combined with *finicky*; for some reason it makes me think of the fact that Prince Charles has a manservant put his toothpaste on his toothbrush every night. That to me is definitively prenzie. A *scamel*, I believe, is just a very rare kind of shellfish—it looks sort of like a purple nautilus, without the tentacles. Or maybe not. No doubt you should come up with your own meaning. Shakespeare must have.

Shakespeare is his words. Lost words, stolen words, fancy words, everyday words, nonsense words, words that trudge through life and words that sing, words like chasms of ever-deepening significance, words that fall apart like sandcastles. He is all of his words, and his words are ours. His truest dominion is in speech, and it grows every time we open our mouths.

THE BEAST WITH
TWO BACKS

From Shakespeare through Freud came the idea that a healthy sex life is an unrepressed sex life. Was there a more powerful, a more vital, a more influential idea in the whole of the twentieth century? Everyone with a penis or a vagina (or both, I guess) has benefited. The sexual revolution of the sixties and the smaller sexual revolution we are undergoing now, with the normalization of homosexuality and every other kind of freakiness, both derive directly from Freud's humanistic, unembarrassed approach to desire. That humanism and that lack of embarrassment are Shakespeare's.

Shakespeare has improved your sex life. If you've had sex without shame, sex for pleasure, for fun, for any reason other than procreation within marriage—Shakespeare, more than any other single figure, is responsible for the climate of permissiveness that made it possible. His frankness about sexuality, even suppressed, has done more to foster open attitudes than any other writer or thinker has.

It's hilarious that we think of ourselves as living in daring sexual times. By the standards of history we are ludicrously hung up. To be honest, I'm not sure I would have had the guts to attend the theater during Shakespeare's time. Not that I'm squeamish—I'll eat sea urchin happily and watch bullfights—but Shakespeare's theater had to compete with the wide range of alternative entertainments available in the London suburbs: Would you rather watch *Hamlet* tonight or a pack of pit bulls ripping a bear apart? Would you rather see *A Midsummer's Night's Dream* or go get hammered and laid? For the right price, you wouldn't have had to choose between prostitutes and a play, because in the most expensive seats female and male hookers conveniently and discreetly serviced clients during performances. You have to admire recent efforts, particularly at the Globe Theatre in London, at reconstructing the original stage setting of Shakespeare's plays, but nobody can re-create the urban atmosphere in which the first productions appeared: much of the audience drunk, hookers flashing their eyes and breasts, the sound of animals in pain, the fear of plague.

Shakespeare was an enthusiastic participant in this festival of carnality. His first hit play was *Titus Andronicus*, a ludicrously savage, grotesque bit of business in which a young woman is raped, her hands and tongue hacked off so that she can't tell anyone. Later, a mother eats her sons baked in a pie. A man is buried alive to be eaten by wild beasts. That play is shocking, I don't care who you are. In 1951, Kenneth Tynan directed an abridged *Titus* at the Irving Theatre in London, and it was so gory and so upsetting that he had to hire St. John Ambulance men to deal with the fallout. "An average of two people, in an audience of just over a hundred, have fainted at each performance," he noted in his production diary. "And last Sunday, to everyone's astonishment, one of the Ambulance men fainted himself." His audience had lived through World War II. They were the same people who survived the Blitz and doodlebugs and D-Day; *Titus Andronicus* made them pass out.

Shakespeare was just as excessive about sex as he was about violence. He saw it everywhere and managed to find lewd puns in music, religion, trade, sports, carpentry, lock-picking, hunting, archery, fishing, war, sailing, farming, mapmaking, all species of animals, and every kind of housework. He managed the most elaborate and complicated dirty jokes ever, such as Mercutio's bit from act 2, scene 1 of *Romeo and Juliet*:

> If love be blind, love cannot hit the mark.
> Now will he sit under a medlar tree
> And wish his mistress were that kind of fruit
> As maids call medlars when they laugh alone.
> O Romeo, that she were, O that she were
> An open-arse, and thou a popp'rin pear.
>
> (2.1.34–39)

You have to know that in Renaissance slang a medlar fruit was known as an open-arse, but once that pun is clear, Mercutio's advice boils down to promoting anal sex.

Shakespeare has become an icon of love poetry— little snatches of his verse are considered perfect for the back of pink heart-shaped boxes or in Valentine's cards attached to roses—even though he wrecked love poetry as it had been known up to his time. In the Petrarchan sonnet, as practiced by Italian poets and by English imitators such as Sir Philip Sidney, the loved one always remains infinitely above the poet. In the traditional love poetry before Shakespeare, the poet rises toward the adored object. The romantic longing for a woman connects with the courtly aspiration to serve the sovereign and the mystical aspiration to serve God, a neatly linked series of unattainable ideals. Shakespeare blew all that to smithereens. Take Sonnet 129:

> The expense of spirit in a waste of shame
> Is lust in action; and till action, lust
> Is perjured, murd'rous, bloody, full of blame,
> Savage, extreme, rude, cruel, not to trust;
> Enjoy'd no sooner but despised straight;
> Past reason hunted; and no sooner had,
> Past reason hated, as a swallow'd bait,
> On purpose laid to make the taker mad:
> Mad in pursuit, and in possession so;
> Had, having, and in quest to have, extreme;
> A bliss in proof, and proved, a very woe;
> Before, a joy proposed; behind, a dream.

All this the world well knows; yet none knows
well
To shun the heaven that leads men to this hell.

Shakespeare replaces the quest for the unattainable ideal with a meditation on semen. He replaces aspiration with the recognition of the material and emotional facts on the ground. Even the sharp shortness of the poem's phrases, chopped up by commas, conveys a rough desire entirely foreign to the languid easiness of a Petrarch or a Sir Philip Sidney. He is uninterested in "How do I reach to touch a star?" It's more like "Why do I always want to go to sleep right after I orgasm?"

Sodomy, fellatio, cunnilingus, prostitution, sex while drunk, sex between men, sex between women, sex alone, sex indoors and outdoors, sex with strangers and between husbands and wives—Shakespeare wrote about it all. He had no time for Puritans and never missed a chance to mock them onstage. Angelo, the self-righteous Duke's deputy in *Measure for Measure* whose job is to clean up the city of Vienna from its overindulgence, amounts to a hypocritical rapist. When Malvolio, a Puritan servant from *Twelfth Night*, picks up a letter from his lady Olivia, he identifies her handwriting with a double entendre, which nobody ever gets when they hear it onstage but is nonetheless hilarious (you have to take *and* as an *n* to get it): "These be her very c's, her u's and her t's, and thus makes she her great P's." He came by his hatred of Puritans honestly. They were trying to destroy his livelihood.

There's no necrophilia or incest in Shakespeare but almost everything else. Transvestitism is always in the background, simply because all the female parts were originally played by boys. Shakespeare used every opportunity to fool around with gender roles. Women fall in love with women dressed like men. Men fall in love with women whom they have known only as men. Sex in Shakespeare's work is fulsome and complicated, his theater a place of opening, thrusting bodies and the mayhem of their consequences. Early audiences loved the bawdiness. During the Restoration, *The Tempest* was considered not bawdy enough, so Dryden added a sexy twin sister for Miranda, named Dorinda, and added some spicy dialogue for her.

Despite being rife with sexuality, Shakespeare is the most cleaned-up author of all time. For most of their lives in performance, Shakespeare's plays had to be mutilated by censors before reaching the stage. At least we get to hear Shakespeare's words when we attend a performance. Speaking the words onstage as they are found in the original sources is a relatively new innovation. Bell's Shakespeare, an edition from 1773, was the first collected version of plays as they were performed on the English stage, and it reveals that the parts of Shakespeare considered decent enough for public performance in the eighteenth century amounted to roughly two-thirds of the original material. In English the word *bowdlerize* has come to mean any act of expurgating and altering texts according to the prudish morality of schoolmarms and tent shouters. Which is profoundly unfair to Thomas and Henrietta Bowdler, the brother-and-sister team who compiled *The Family Shakespeare* in 1807 and earned themselves that infamy through the enormous popularity of their edition. In context, the Bowdlers were far from prudes. They were cutting far less material than was typically cut at the theater.

The Bowdlers were at least honest about their cutting. *Othello* was the ultimate nightmare for a delicate sensibility such as Thomas Bowdler's—hot sex with a black dude—yet the man was intelligent and forthright enough to recognize the play couldn't be bowdlerized: "This tragedy is justly considered as one of the noblest efforts of dramatic genius that has appeared in any age or in any language; but the subject is unfortunately little suited to family reading." The initial reaction to *The Family Shakespeare* was indignation that anyone could consider Shakespeare, in any form, proper reading for young ladies or children.

You have only to compare the *Othello* in *The Family Shakespeare* to the one put out a few years earlier by the Reverend James Plumtre in *The English Drama Purified* to see that the Bowdlers were restorers rather than destroyers. Plumtre didn't just alter the language or clip a few characters. He turned the play into a comedy. Instead of a stunned crowd of onlookers watching Othello commit suicide over his murdered wife's corpse, the servant rouses Desdemona in the end:

> My mistress' fame is clear'd: her innocence
> Is pure and spotless as the driven snow.
> *Othello.* O my much injur'd, dearest Desdemona,
> How can I dare to look thee in the face,
> How hope forgiveness ever can be mine?

Even the wildest avant-garde adapter of today is more true to Shakespeare than the majority of his stodgy predecessors—which director alive would have the nerve to turn *Othello* into a comedy?

By the middle of the nineteenth century, expurgated versions of Shakespeare had spread so widely and thoroughly that it became possible to imagine Shakespeare without sex. As Britain became an empire, Shakespeare became a secular, sexless saint. The sonnets became Platonic love poems, not weird sexual fascinations. A comparison with Dante is illuminating. The national poet of Italy had a sex life overwhelmed by an unrequited longing for a virginal girl, and yet he grew in the nineteenth century into a byword for passion. Shakespeare, from what evidence we have, screwed around in the broadest sense of the word, and yet his followers turned him into an incorporeal spirit, totally divorced from matters of the body. The classical bust that makes him look like the well-fed middle-class shopkeeping English ideal became the best-known image of Shakespeare.

This is not the statue of a sex god. W. H. Auden wrote, in his memorial poem for W. B. Yeats, that "the words of a dead man are modified in the guts of the living." Their

The wooden bust of Shakespeare in Stratford-upon-Avon.

bodies are modified, too, in the image of the nations that assume them as icons.

Shakespeare's plays are the most repressed in history, and that has been his most enduring contribution to sex: he's the missing sexy stuff that everybody knows is missing. The collected plays are second only to the Bible as the ultimate establishment text—the morality police couldn't avoid him even as they couldn't accept him. Just as every schoolboy who studies Latin learns eventually about the dirty stuff in Catullus, so every literate schoolboy caught rumors about unexpurgated Shakespeare. *Psst* . . . Check out *The Winter's Tale*, act 4, scene 4, line 197 (she's buying a dildo). Or Sonnet 135 (an ode to his own prick). Or *Cymbeline*, act 2, scene 3, line 13 (he's fingering her and then eating her out).

Sigmund Freud was the most educated, most curious, and most important dirty schoolboy who ever lived, and he knew all the spots in Shakespeare. Sex without sentimentality, without the miasma of religion, without morality; sex considered simply as a reality with which human beings grapple—this shift in thinking was the most fundamental sexual revolution of the twentieth century and the forerunner of all the others. Freud's frankness was his greatest achievement. It changed the private life of the twentieth century. It changed your life. And Freud's major source was Shakespeare.

"Canst thou not minister to a mind diseased?" Macbeth begs his wife's doctor; "Therein the patient must minister to himself," the doctor replies. Psychoanalysis is a practice of which Shakespeare himself could never have conceived, and yet he gave birth to it. The great literary critic Harold Bloom is undoubtedly correct that psychoanalysis is Shakespeare prosified. Freud's earliest insights about the workings of the psyche derive from two sources: Shakespeare and himself. He didn't feel he needed any others. In *Hamlet*, Freud found the ultimate confirmation for his theory of the Oedipus complex—the fundamental human desire to kill one's father and sleep with one's mother. In the original Greek tragedy, that desire is expressed openly. In *Hamlet* it's hidden, repressed. For Freud, the repression of the Oedipus complex is the basic motive of human history, explaining both private and public actions. Hamlet is the original neurotic and we are all neurotics.

The Oedipus complex is the most important concept in psychoanalysis because its repression has the most dramatic consequences in everyday life. We repress our desires—we have to—and they return to haunt us like the Ghost that haunts Elsinore. Repressed desires have to be uncovered and dealt with so that they do not return in unpredictable and terrifying manifestations. It's why people go to shrinks. There is a moral to *Hamlet* in Freud's reading: It's better to sleep with Ophelia than murder her dad in your mom's bedroom.

More than Freud's conclusions, though, more than the methods he applied to human psychology, Freud's importance is in the assumptions underpinning his conclusions and methodology: that human sexuality can be studied and that recognition of its reality is a humanizing pleasure. These assumptions derive directly from a reading of Shakespeare. Sonnet 129 above is a personal case study of the effect of orgasm. It is Shakespeare's self-analysis, showing the way to all the other self-analyses. It's not just that Freud would never have existed without Shakespeare. Psychology as a field of human endeavor would never have been possible without him.

Fittingly, Shakespeare's plays have been major beneficiaries in the Freudian revolution in sex. Well into the twentieth century, directors and critics ignored the cross-dressing aspect of his theater, arguing that young boys playing women were a convention and so nobody would have noticed. With the coming of the sexual revolution, this absurd idea vanished. How can you play *Twelfth Night*, with a woman dressed as a man (who is really a man dressed as a woman) and a woman falling in love with a woman who is dressed as a man (who is really a man) without taking into account the charged effect of its role-bending sexuality? Doing a transvestite performance of this play is evidence not of a political agenda but of an authenticity agenda. The plays are crammed with homoerotic desire. However, it is not homoerotic desire *as opposed to* heterosexual desire. Sex is an action, rather than an identity, in Shakespeare. Having sex with a member of your own gender would not have defined the soul of the person doing it.

We are nearly back to the full and omnivorous sexuality of Shakespeare's world, in which what you do in the bedroom is part of you but does not define your person. The most recent sexual survey of America, from Indiana University's Center for Sexual Health Promotion in 2010, paints a remarkably freaky picture of daily American life. Forty percent of women age 20–24 have had anal sex. Oral sex is now a commonplace; nearly 90 percent of participants in the survey had performed it in the last month. Whereas only 8 percent of men identified as gay, 15 percent had experimented. People still giggle at the Wednesday matinees of *Measure for Measure*, when some adventurous director chooses to start the play off with seedy Viennese strippers. But more and more, sex is an integral part of Shakespeare productions, and sometimes the focus. *The Donkey Show* in New York stages *A Midsummer Night's Dream* in a seventies-style disco, complete with classic dance tunes, nudity, and drugs. I'll leave you to guess the salient Donkeyesque feature of the star performer. Women go to the play for stagette parties.

Shakespeare represents humanity, fully and frankly, which means that he does not look away from the dirty bits. Anyone who wants to know him, no matter how prudish or how repressed or how censorious, has to accept that the dirty bits are there, that the dirty bits are a part of the whole of life. This frankness is one of Shakespeare's most important gifts to history.

Sometimes I wonder what Shakespeare would think if, for a brief moment, he were allowed to walk around in our time. Most of the world would be bewildering,

I'm sure—what could he possibly make of me watching *Hamlet* on my iPad on a transatlantic flight? Skyscrapers? Telephones? Half-African presidents of the United States? None of it would make any sense. Our sex lives would not surprise him, though. If anything, he would find our vaunted openness a bit backward. Why make such a big deal out of simple bodily matters? He would have loved the nubile women and the huge swinging penis in *The Donkey Show* for sure. A man who spent his life in the London suburbs of the 1600s would feel completely at home at Studio 54.

He changed sex. Every other change—the iPad, the airplanes, the skyscrapers—is nothing beside it.

FLAMING YOUTH

Shakespeare described the terrifying beauty of the adolescent so early in its development, and so definitively and so thoroughly, that it is only slightly an exaggeration to say that he invented teenagers as we know them today. *Romeo and Juliet*, his extended study of the humiliations and glories of adolescence, is the biggest hit of all time; everybody knows the story even if they haven't seen the play. Just one year after its first performance in 1596, the Quarto publication proclaimed that "it hath been often (with great applause) plaid publiquely." Unlike most of Shakespeare's plays, it has never slipped out of fashion. *Hamlet*—Shakespeare's other great play about adolescence—is the only piece performed more regularly onstage, and when you consider how often and how successfully *Romeo and Juliet* has been adapted into other media, into operas and ballets and musicals, its popularity is even more staggering. The most popular brand of Cuban cigars? *Romeo y Julietta*. People just love to watch a couple of dumb kids make out and die. And they are awfully young, these dumb Veronese kids who make out for us and then die. Shakespeare doesn't ever tell us Romeo's exact age, but we know about Juliet. In the first act, her nurse discusses her age at length, and it's creepy. In two weeks she will be fourteen. To anyone other than Polish film directors, thirteen may seem a tad young for the beginning of a love affair. But surely the eternal question of adolescence is just that: How young is too young?

Teenagers are upsetting. There they are, smoking outside crumbling schools or hunched over their cell phones in the doorway of the Gap, texting while walking, making out in groups under elm trees in the park, scowling at passing motorists from under skeleton-print hoodies, everywhere discomfiting and magnificent. What could be more gorgeous or more hideous than teenagers? With their awkward lovely bodies, their flawed and yet more than perfect skin, their arrogance and their vulnerability, a welter of deep carnal urgings and swiftly turning, sudden, unpredictable intellectual growth, they're even more confusing in groups. One recent September, having a drink with an older and wiser university colleague at a bar overrun with frosh partiers, I wondered aloud how anyone survives adolescence. "They're all so beautiful and they think they're so ugly," she answered. To which I added after a few more drinks: "They're all so ignorant and they think they know everything."

Young love is the world's most intoxicating stuff. The teen idol of the moment, Justin Bieber, uses up 3 percent of Twitter's entire server capacity. Youth sells perfume, clothes, movies, music, drinks, everything. The world's most expensive and popular models are just barely pubescent—the sexiest women's clothes look best on girls with whom it would be illegal to have sex. Teenagers live in a state of maximum desirability as well as maximum contempt. They are in an impossible position— impossible to others and to themselves.

The great French scholar Philippe Ariès, in his monumental study of the subject, concluded that for most of the Medieval period "people had no idea of what we call adolescence, and the idea was a long time taking shape."

In England, in the late fifteenth century, the normal thing to do with your kids was to send them, at the age of eight or nine, to serve as apprentices in somebody else's house. It wasn't a matter of class. The rich as well as the poor wanted their children to serve masters, in order to learn manners. The connection between youth and servitude survives linguistically in French—they still call a waiter a *garçon*. But by the end of the fifteenth century, adolescence morphed, according to Ariès, through "a slow and profound revolution, scarcely distinguished by either contemporary observers or later historians, and difficult to recognize." From a state of servitude, adolescence was transformed into a period of exploration and freedom. Ariès attributes the change to the rise of colleges in Western Europe. Complaints about the disorder and moral quagmire of such colleges began almost immediately after they sprang up. From the beginning the question was "how do we civilize these brutes?"

The opening scene of *Romeo and Juliet* shows young men terrorizing the streets of Verona with instantly recognizable teenage nastiness: Stupid jokes, stupid bragging, stupid sexism, stupid violence, and stupid loyalty follow one another so quickly that the audience is barely given enough time to hate the young men for one failing before another rushes in to take its place. They remind me exactly of a group of teenagers I saw once at a football game: punching each other repeatedly, drunk, farting in each other's faces, describing an overweight girl as "more cushion for the pushin'," totally gross. These boys didn't just resemble Samson and Gregory from act 1, scene 1 of *Romeo and Juliet*. They were identical. Pseudo-gangsters. The uncanniness of the play is that it has managed to be exactly like each new crop of teenagers for four hundred years.

What exactly is a teenager anyway? The difficulty we have categorizing them is surely a huge part of why we fear them. Even the most precise language—the language of the law—can't decide one way or the other. In the United States, a nineteen-year-old is not mature enough to consume alcohol but is quite mature enough to survive the physical and moral nightmares of war. When I was eighteen, I would frequently fly from the East Coast of Canada, where the drinking age is nineteen, to my family home in Alberta, where the legal limit is eighteen. Sometimes the stewardess would let me drink on the flight and sometimes not. It depended on which side of the country she was stationed out of. Sex only renders the problem of

Charlotte Cushman as Romeo with her sister Susan as Juliet.

categorization more urgent. In Georgia, North Carolina, and Florida, the legislatures have recently passed laws that allow judges to forgo mandatory sentences for teenagers who have been caught having sex with each other. By the letter of the law, a relationship between, say, a fourteen-year-old and a sixteen-year-old would constitute statutory rape and bear the minimum sentence of ten years. The "rapist" would have a record as a sexual offender, forced to declare his or her criminality to new neighbors after every move. Fortunately these three states have had the good sense to recognize that adolescence cannot and will not fit into such neat boxes. The new laws are called, naturally, the "Romeo and Juliet provisions."

Romeo and Juliet carries all this adolescent baggage and dumps it in a heap on the stage. Even finding age-appropriate actors to play the parts is a substantial problem. To find a teenage actor with the necessary skill for Romeo is nearly impossible. The first Romeo, Richard Burbage, could make do with his midtwenties looks. The first Juliet, as with all the women's parts in Shakespeare's theater, would have been played by a boy. To find a thirteen-year-old girl to play Juliet today is possibly illegal. So even to look at the bodies of the actors and believe them to be the bodies of the characters, we are forced to fudge a little. Mature male actors in the nineteenth century refused to play Romeo, finding him too boyish, and their reluctance proved an opportunity for female actresses such as the great Charlotte Cushman, who played opposite her sister Susan's Juliet in 1846.

Romeo and Juliet has to be fudged. In the eighteenth century, David Garrick understood that his audience wanted a pure and innocent *Romeo and Juliet*, and he gave them a sentimentalized version of the play, which was so much to their liking that his version survived intact for over a century. To make the young lovers totally heroic, he had to make them less complicated—the first thing to go was Romeo's love for Rosaline at the beginning of the play. Romeo's mooning over another girl is embarrassing to everybody; he seems unreliable, and it's a bit insulting to Juliet. Garrick's audience wanted Romeo and Juliet to be proper first lovers. He gave the audience what it wanted. He also fiddled with several lines, in order to remove, in his words, "the Jingle and Quibble which were always thought a great objection to performing it." He cut the dirty jokes, like Mercutio's pun about anal sex in the first act. And he also cut down on the rhyming—it made the lovers seem too silly and too unrealistic. The biggest change, however, was the death scene. Garrick let Juliet wake up before Romeo is properly dead—a flamboyant effect that is not in the original.

Garrick created teenagers who were icons of purity in a corrupt adult world. But Shakespeare, unlike Garrick, never spares his adolescent lovers their ridiculousness. The first snatch of dialogue between Romeo and Juliet is beautiful and absurd. Notice that the dialogue follows the rhyme pattern of a Shakespearean sonnet.

> ROMEO: If I profane with my unworthiest hand
> This holy shrine, the gentle sin is this,
> My lips, two blushing pilgrims, ready stand
> To smooth that rough touch with a tender kiss.
> JULIET: Good pilgrim, you do wrong your hand
> too much,
> Which mannerly devotion shows in this,
> For saints have hands that pilgrims' hands do
> touch,
> And palm to palm is holy palmers' kiss.
> ROMEO: Have not saints lips, and holy palmers
> too?

JULIET: Ay, pilgrim, lips that they must use in
    prayer.
ROMEO: O then, dear saint, let lips do what
    hands do;
They pray, grant thou, lest faith turn to despair.
JULIET: Saints do not move, though grant for
    prayer's sake.
ROMEO: Then move not, while my prayer's effect
    I take.

They kiss.
Thus from my lips, by thine, my sin is purged.
JULIET: Then have my lips the sin that they have
    took.
ROMEO: Sin from my lips? O trespass sweetly urged!
    Give me my sin again.

He kisses her.
JULIET: You kiss by the book.

(1.4.206–223)

The vague but palpable effect of this sudden advent of
ABAB CDCD EFEF GG rhyme is inexplicable beauty.
Only the sharpest members of the audience could conceiv-

ably be sharp enough to notice that the lovers have dipped into sonnet form, but Shakespeare leaves us with an inarticulate impression that the young lovers are somehow strange and magical. Garrick took the sonnet out of the scene exactly because it made their love seem too ridiculous and artificial. But Shakespeare *wants* them ridiculous. That's how kids are. And the last line is perfect: "You kiss by the book." It sounds to me exactly like what a thirteen-year-old girl says after a first kiss, like she's been kissing forever, like she knows all about kissing, like she's read the book.

Romeo and Juliet are beautiful not despite their absurdity but because of it. Romeo may have begun the play in a maddeningly silly love for Rosaline, but he's so much better than his rival Paris, the fine upstanding square who wants to buy Juliet like so much pastry. The mature adults of the play come off poorly on all points. They treat sexuality as exchange, a deal made in the interests of family and society, a matter for the cold calculation of property and propriety. Even the violence of the younger members of both families is better than the viciousness of their elders. The kids may be absurd, but the rationality of their parents is worse.

Nothing could seem more natural to us than the rebellion of teenagers, which explains why *Romeo and Juliet* has fit easily into twentieth-century pop culture. Irving Berlin referred to the pair in a bunch of different songs, as have Bob Dylan, Bruce Springsteen, Madonna, Tom Waits, Dire Straits, Alanis Morissette, Aerosmith, Elvis Costello, and the Indigo Girls. Lou Reed's *Romeo Had Juliette* is a surprisingly conservative retelling of the story. On the street, the young crack dealers dream of automatic weapons, random murder, and the decline of Western civilization. Inside, Romeo clutches a cross and Juliet. The young in Lou Reed's song are the harbingers of apocalyptic social decay, and their only redemption is in the love they preserve against the despair everywhere around them.

In *The Wild One*, a woman at a bar asks Marlon Brando what he's rebelling against. "Whaddaya got?" he slurs back. The teenage rebel cannot say: "I'm rebelling against an inefficient health care system," or "I believe that the incidental tax rate is too high for local corporations," or "our agribusiness policies are shortsighted." No. That would not be nearly stupid or grand enough. The most important feature of adolescent rebellion is that it's doomed. It must come to an end. In this, as well, Shakespeare was right there at the beginning. He defined what it means to be "star-cross'd." The opposition between the adolescent and the mature orders of the world can have only two possible endings. One is comic: The teenager grows up, develops a sense of humor, gets married, has kids, moves to the suburbs, gets fat, and becomes boring. That's what happens to most Romeos and Juliets. The other is tragic: The teenager blows up in a blaze of glory. We much prefer to live the comedy. We much prefer to watch the tragedy.

God, we love to watch young people be destroyed. We crave it. That's why we have gossip magazines, so we can watch Lindsay Lohan and Britney Spears and the Olsen twins self-destruct. Even by the mid-eighteenth century, performances of *Romeo and Juliet* had become excuses for elaborate funeral scenes. The Covent Garden *Romeo and Juliet* in 1750 required a procession, which included the following, among other mourners: trumpeters, drummers, flautists, six children in gray caps with blue bands, and an entire choir. Such onstage funerals were realistic enough to inspire discomfort in foreign visitors whenever they were performed. It seemed so profane to imitate religious ceremonies so closely. But English audiences loved them and continue to love them. Zefferelli put a long Juliet funeral in his film version of 1963.

Directors and long-suffering stage managers had to add the funeral to *Romeo and Juliet* but not to *Hamlet*, in which Ophelia's death and burial are key moments of the action. I should admit right out that most scholars would never think of *Hamlet* as a play about adolescence. Hamlet is obviously no teenager. He has traditionally been played by an actor in his midthirties, although the play can be confusing about how old Hamlet is. Horatio, his fellow student at Wittenburg, states clearly that he was at the battle where the king of Denmark slew Fortinbras's father. In the fifth act, one of the gravediggers informs us that Hamlet was born on that day. Which doesn't make any sense. Even Shakespeare makes mistakes.

Is it possible that Hamlet, while not a teenager, is nonetheless an adolescent? The times in which I live make this eventuality seem eminently plausible to me. I have met many, many men in their midfifties who are still unsure what they're going to do with their lives. Generation X is still Generation X, even though they're much closer to the end of life than the beginning.

At any rate, Hamlet is in love with Ophelia, the enduring icon of female adolescence and of the potential self-destruction it entails. *Reviving Ophelia* is the perfect name for a self-help book about teenage girls, even if the book does make only one reference to the play. Ophelia has become an icon of adolescence exactly because she has been denied adolescence. Her father and her brother and her king and her lover push her around constantly. She has no room to play or to explore. She's in the same situation as Juliet, whose first line is, "How now, who calls?" At least Juliet has Romeo as an avenue for escape.

Ophelia's lack of control over her death is even more complete than her lack of control over her life. She allows herself to be drowned by her clothes. Even her suicide is a passive act. The famous graveyard scene in *Hamlet*, with Yorick's skull, contains two full-length discussions of the theological ramifications of her burial in consecrated ground—one from clowns and one from priests. Then Hamlet and Laertes jump in her grave to fight. (Even her grave is a place only for other people's opinions. Even her rotting corpse is an opportunity for somebody else's expression. Even dead, she serves others.) Her death happens offstage, described by Gertrude in a lyric pastoral.

There is a willow grows aslant a brook
That shows his hoar leaves in the glassy stream.
There with fantastic garlands did she come.
Of crow-flowers, nettles, daisies, and long purples
That liberal shepherds give a grosser name,
But our cold maids do dead men's fingers call them.
There on the pendent boughs her coronet weeds
Clambering to hang, an envious sliver broke;
When down the weedy trophies and herself
Fell in the weeping brook. Her clothes spread wide,
And mermaid-like awhile they bore her up;
Which time she chanted snatches of old tunes,
As one incapable of her own distress,
Or like a creature native and endued
Unto that element. But long it could not be
Till that her garments, heavy with their drink,
Pulled the poor wretch from her melodious lay
To muddy death.

(4.7.164–181)

The passage is doubly creepy: Ophelia allows herself to be dragged down to death, and Gertrude, who describes it all in precise detail, seems to have seen the entire thing without trying to help. Ophelia's death is not quite suicide but not quite an accident either. She failed to stop nature from killing her. She let herself go into death, "incapable of her own distress."

The iconography of the self-smothered young woman is a perennial favorite. Pictures of Ophelia have been a constant in English art from the time *Hamlet* was first staged. When Julia Margaret Cameron started taking photographs in the 1850s, she dressed her relatives as Ophelia. Here's her niece, Julia Jackson:

Think about that: She dressed her favorite nieces up in flowers to look like an emotionally abused semi-suicide. Millais's famous painting has to be the most powerful Ophelia of the Victorian era, though.

In Millais's vision, the young woman is dragged to her death by the water's weight on her hips. As nature overwhelms her—and the painting is more a work of landscape than portraiture—the look on her face is one of pure sexual ecstasy. Being subsumed by nature is a replacement for being subsumed by sex. A deep well of unexpressed longing rises from her physical repression—the ideal of adolescent womanhood in Victorian England. Which is maybe why Julia Margaret Cameron could feel comfortable dressing up her nieces to look like a suicide—she wanted them to allow themselves to be smothered.

Gregory Crewdson's twenty-first-century Ophelia is an homage to Millais, and also an inversion.

Nature is not overwhelming this young woman. A suburban life of blandness and boredom has already killed her. She is floating on the water's surface rather than drowning, but Millais and Crewdson are describing the same condition. Both of their young women are unable to

Millais's Ophelia is weighted down by water.

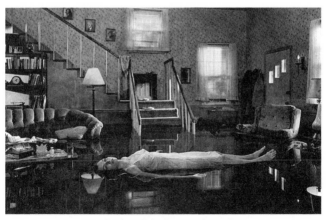

Crewdson's Ophelia floats on the surface.

find self-expression and achieve it only in a kind of half-silent gasp in death.

What could be more different than the lives of young women in Victorian England and twenty-first-century America? And yet both Crewdson and Millais turn to the iconography of Ophelia. That is how strong and low and powerful the silent river of Shakespeare's influence runs. We think that we interpret *Romeo and Juliet* or *Hamlet* but actually they interpret us. Our whole understanding of adolescence is there to be found in him—and perhaps a deeper understanding than our current mixture of envy and loathing. Shakespeare loves his teenagers even as he paints them in all their absurdity and nastiness. That basic honesty, neither idealizing nor afraid, has kept *Romeo and Juliet* fresh. Leonardo DiCaprio and Claire Danes became the dominant young actors of their generation through their performances in Baz Luhrmann's *Romeo + Juliet.* Justin Bieber, with his swagger coach and overwhelming fame, comes appropriately from Stratford, the home of North America's biggest Shakespeare festival.

Shakespeare created this category of humanity, which now seems as organic to us as the spring. In place of nostalgia and loathing, Shakespeare would have us look at teenagers in a spirit of wonder, even the spotty ones and the awkward ones and the wild ones. They're us before we fall into categories: not children, not adults, not monsters, not saints. They're beautiful because they do not fit. They're too much themselves and not enough.

ALL HONORABLE MEN

Now I want to tell you a murder mystery, a murder mystery that is also a ghost story. You may feel that you already have the solution to this particular problem: Who killed Abraham Lincoln? It was John Wilkes Booth, we all know, who stalked into Ford's Theatre, raised the gun, and fired the bullet. But the Lincoln assassination was more than a scene that could have been written by Shakespeare. In many ways it *was* a scene written by Shakespeare. The terms of the assassination were all set out in *Julius Caesar*.

A night at the theater can change us. It's hard to say how or why, but a good play can sometimes transform who we are. In our time, politicians and the editors of the op-ed pages casually assume a causal link between culture and violence, that music and books and video games make our world either more civilized or more dangerous. The corollary to this assumption is the widely held belief that we live in uniquely violent times. Nothing could be further from the truth. Think Grand Theft Auto is violent? For most of human history, dog-fighting has been among the more popular pastimes. Executions used to be public entertainment. When they captured the poisoner Cardozo during the reign of Elizabeth I, the executioners didn't just hang him. They hanged him slowly, so that his neck wouldn't break. Then they cut off his testicles, removed his internal organs one by one, hacked his body into quarters, and piled up the pieces at the south end of London Bridge. The crowds loved it. After the Gunpowder Plot of 1605, the spectators enjoyed burning Guy Fawkes so much, they decided to do it every year.

Julius Caesar, as an entertainment, isn't that far from dogfighting or effigy burning. Everybody who attends the play is there to witness the killing of a great man. The conspirators bathe themselves in Caesar's blood, at Brutus's orders.

Stoop, Romans, stoop,
And let us bathe our hands in Caesar's blood
Up to the elbows, and besmear our swords:
Then walk we forth, even to the market-place,
And waving our red weapons o'er our heads,
Let's all cry, "Peace, freedom, and liberty!"

(3.1.105–110)

The play is a bloodbath. *Julius Caesar*'s climax is a brutal killing in the coldest blood, which stains the pure white marble of the ancient Roman Capitol building. That building, the synecdoche of republicanism, should be the ultimate symbol of the terrors of physical violence sublimated into the civilities of debate. Instead it's a butcher's block.

The murder mystery and ghost story I have to tell is also a story about two brothers and their reactions to the bloodbath of *Julius Caesar*. The lives of both famous Booth brothers were inextricably entwined with the play: Edwin Booth used it to become one of the greatest performers of his generation; John Wilkes Booth used it to assassinate the president of the United States. Both became great actors, though in different senses of the phrase.

November 25, 1864, New York. A night that crystallized the history of American violence into a single delirious allegory. While General Tecumseh Sherman's campaign in Georgia was introducing total warfare to the modern world, Southern partisans burned hotels along Broadway—the first instance of domestic terrorism on American soil. They spread burning phosphorus on the beds at the Saint James, the Lafarge, the Metropolitan, the Brandreth, Frenche's, and the Belmont. They even torched Barnum's Museum. While Broadway was burning, at the Winter Garden Theatre, the Booths, onstage together for the first time, performed Shakespeare's *Julius Caesar* as a benefit to raise money for a Shakespeare statue in Central Park. It's the statue that still stands on the Literary Walk, smeared with starling feces.

In retelling the Caesar story as it is found in Plutarch, Shakespeare was working at his most topical, feeding on the most widespread political fear of his time, that Queen Elizabeth would be assassinated. Much like Caesar, Elizabeth in the later years of her reign was converting herself into a kind of semi-deity—the Fairy Queen, Gloriana— but unlike Caesar, she was quite aware of how many people wanted to kill her. Queen Elizabeth never married and produced no heirs. Her death would have meant chaos, and there were many people interested in chaos, from all sides of the political spectrum. Protestant splinter groups were proposing entirely separate religious organizations, and Catholics were all set to replace Elizabeth with a monarch of their own faith. Her death would have meant civil war, and as America found out two and a half centuries later, civil war is the worst disaster that can befall a country, worse than being conquered, worse than plague. By law, every church in England every Sunday had to read one of the state-sanctioned homilies, which reiterated on a regular basis how unacceptable any violence against "the Lord's anointed" would be. Elizabeth, as well as Shakespeare, knew how to use the potential of her grisly murder for dramatic effect. In 1588, without bodyguards, she walked out to address the sailors setting off to fight the Spanish Armada: "Let tyrants fear," she told the crowd. "I have so behaved myself that under God I have placed my chiefest strength and safeguard in the loyal hearts and good will of my subjects." No doubt Shakespeare remembered this moment when he imagined Caesar striding fearlessly into the arms of his betrayers.

The threat of national dissolution hung thickly over America in 1864, as it did over England in 1599. Edwin and John Wilkes were both patriots, but their opinions on the Civil War could not have been more divided. When Edwin's wife gave birth to their first son in London, he draped the Stars and Stripes over the birthing bed so that his son wouldn't be born under a foreign flag. Union was sacred to him. John Wilkes had been born and raised on the family farm in Maryland, where he developed loyalty to the South and its institutions, including slavery. So far, so typical. What could be more natural than brothers disagreeing about the major political questions of the day? I can almost hear the screaming over Thanksgiving dinner.

More than politics, what divided the Booth brothers was also what connected them, their father Junius Brutus Booth, whom many considered the finest actor of his generation. His name split them up. Because of his widespread renown, audiences would happily pay to watch his actor sons, but each one had to stake out a different territory: Edwin took the Northeast, John Wilkes the South, and Junius Brutus Jr., the third brother, took the West. Even their names fit eerily into the themes of *Julius*

John Wilkes Booth and his brothers in Julius Caesar.

Caesar. The original Lucius Junius Brutus was Brutus's most famous ancestor, the man who kicked the kings out of Rome and served as one of the first two consuls. It was Lucius Junius Brutus who invented the oath that all consuls took, the oath swearing never to permit kings in Rome. He was a man so steeped in duty that he sentenced his own sons to death for failing to fulfill their military duty. John Wilkes was a great English champion of liberty from the eighteenth century. Even without Shakespeare, the Booth brothers knew in their very names the staggering weight of tradition behind the story of the murder of Caesar. They knew that Brutus inherited the expectations of his glorious forefathers in the pursuit of liberty.

The Booth boys were trying to live up to Daddy's name just like the original Brutus—John Wilkes by becoming a tyrant-slayer, and Edwin by becoming a great actor. For John Wilkes, the theater was a place that stirred ghosts, that brought demons into the world, and he became one of these demons. For Edwin, the theater was a place to bring in the ghosts, to comfort and assuage them. The day after the Booth brothers benefit, Edwin went on to open in *Hamlet* on Broadway, a production that ran for a then-record one hundred days. John Wilkes went on to assassinate Lincoln.

April 9, 1865, Washington. Lincoln was drifting up the Potomac on a steamship with Senator Charles Sumner, his wife, and a small group of friends. For several hours, the president read aloud from *Macbeth*, concentrating on his favorite passages from the scenes immediately before Macbeth has murdered King Duncan. He must, at some point, have discussed the speech from act 1, scene 7:

> If it were done when 'tis done, then 'twere well
> It were done quickly: if the assassination
> Could trammel up the consequences, and catch
> With his surcease success; that but this blow
> Might be the be-all and the end-all here,
> But here, upon this bank and shoal of time,
> We'ld jump the life to come.

> (1.7.1–7)

It is a great speech of prevarication: surcease matched with success, be-all with end-all, bank with shoal. The language teeter-totters, the talk of a man who hasn't made up his mind, who doesn't want to make up his mind. John

Wilkes by all accounts did not prevaricate. He fulfilled what he undertook, like Brutus. This speech marks the first use of the word *assassination* in the English language, so the man who was to be the first assassinated president likely spent some of his last hours contemplating the first usage of the word that would define his legacy. History allows itself these sick jokes from time to time.

Washington in 1865 was nothing like ancient Rome. It lacked many of the chintzy imperial imitations that fill the capital today. The streets ran with thick yellow mud, and the whole city had not developed much from its original swampland. The city was a human swamp as well. The conspirators who plotted the assassination of the president shared little with their noble Roman antecedents; they planned their squalid little murder in a squalid little rooming house, and Booth alone among them had the fortitude to take their decision to its ultimate conclusion. He, too, was definitely a down-market tyrannicide. The main similarity between Caesar's murder and Lincoln's was the flamboyant theatricality of the assassinations.

April 14, 1865, Good Friday. Ford's Theatre was showing *Our American Cousin*, by Tom Taylor. The president's box was conspicuously placed several feet above the other viewers, spectacularly adorned with flags and a portrait of Washington. The presence of the president was part of the entertainment. One of the big jokes in the show had to be changed because Lincoln had recently canceled the much-hated draft. The lead female character, Georgina, asks to be moved away from a window. Without the president in the box, her opposite, Dundreary, is supposed to reply: "Oh, you want to get out of the draft do you? Well, you're not the only one who wants to escape the draft." With the president in the building, though, Dundreary says "You are mistaken. The draft has already been stopped by order of the President!"

John Wilkes Booth understood the theatrical value of that stage box. As he crept up behind Lincoln, he waited for the line "I guess I know enough to turn you inside out, old gal—you sockdologizing old man-trap." (And we may wonder if he even had in mind all the possible connotations of *man-trap* as a word for Lincoln to die on? He shot Lincoln on Good Friday. Was the crucifix a man-trap? Was the war the man-trap? Was he himself the man-trap?) John Wilkes Booth fired during the huge burst of laughter the line always provoked, then leaped onto the stage, shouted "*Sic semper tyrannis*"—"Thus ever to tyrants"—and fled. (In *Julius Caesar*, at the moment of crisis, Caesar bursts into Latin—*et tu, Brute*.) Booth fled through the back exit into an alley. Several reports claim that he was immediately followed by J. B. Stewart, the tallest man in Washington, pursuing the assassin like the ghost of Lincoln. (As the ghost of Caesar pursues Brutus.)

April 15, 1865. When the news of his brother's deed reached Edwin in Boston, he canceled all his theatrical engagements. His career as an actor, he believed, was over—the distinction of his father's name, through which he had been promoted, was instantly extinguished by the new infamy of his brother. John Wilkes's career as an assassin was also ending, but not before he managed to scribble: "After being hunted like a dog through swamps, woods, and last night being chased by gun-boats till I was forced to return wet cold and starving, with every man's hand against me, I am here in despair. And why? For doing what Brutus was honoured for."

His pursuers caught him at the Garrett farm, burned him out, shot him, and buried his corpse beneath the floor of a Washington penitentiary.

It's tempting to believe that John Wilkes was insane. So his family claimed. But he was certainly sane enough to understand *Julius Caesar.* At the Shakespeare benefit, he played Marc Antony, the avenger of assassination. He gave the famous speech—high school teachers use it to introduce their sarcastic students to the concept of irony—in which Antony repeats, with increasing contempt, "Brutus is an honourable man."

> Friends, Romans, countrymen, lend me your
>   ears;
> I come to bury Caesar, not to praise him.
> The evil that men do lives after them,
> The good is oft interred with their bones;
> So let it be with Caesar. The noble Brutus
> Hath told you Caesar was ambitious.
> If it were so, it was a grievous fault,
> And grievously hath Caesar answer'd it.
> Here, under leave of Brutus and the rest,
> (For Brutus is an honourable man,
> So are they all, all honourable men)
> Come I to speak in Caesar's funeral.

> (3.2.75–86)

The brilliance of Antony's irony must not have been lost on Booth. In the next scene, Antony is shown calmly listing enemies to have murdered. There are two levels of irony in the speech. Antony says that Brutus is noble meaning that he is not, but he always knows that Brutus is "the noblest Roman of them all." Shakespeare's tragic vision encompassed the truth of a contradiction. Brutus has to kill Caesar. Then Brutus must, in turn, be killed. John Wilkes Booth was a better interpreter of *Julius Caesar* than his brother Edwin. He took his interpretation into the world.

A little less than a year after John Wilkes assassinated Lincoln, Edwin was able to act again. He returned as Hamlet, the most successful Hamlet of his generation, one of the greatest Hamlets of all time. The history of his tortured family added to the power of his performances. His audiences all thought of him as a haunted man. In 1871, he dared to try *Julius Caesar*, and in that production he created the characterization—commonly adopted by later actors—that Brutus is reluctant about the murder. At the moment of assassination, Cassius tears Caesar from the throne and stabs him with great pleasure. Brutus, as the stage notes tell us, "turns away in revulsion."

It's hard to find textual evidence to support revulsion on the part of Brutus (though there are rumors in Plutarch that Brutus was secretly Caesar's son). In an early scene, after the conspirators break up for morning, Brutus has trouble rousing his slave boy.

> Boy! Lucius! Fast asleep? It is no matter;
> Enjoy the honey-heavy dew of slumber:
> Thou hast no figures nor no fantasies
> Which busy care draws in the brains of men;
> Therefore thou sleep'st so sound.

> (2.1.229-233)

But he doesn't waver from his decision at any point. He bathes in blood. The revulsion is more Booth than Shakespeare. What was Edwin turning away from? Was it Brutus turning away from his forefathers? Or Edwin turning away from his brother? Was he turning away from the whole spectacle of violence? From murder itself? From Junius Brutus or from Caesar? From Lincoln or from John Wilkes? Or was he turning himself into the ghost of his brother to relive again and again the crime that spread outward agonizingly and without limit?

The best murder mysteries are always ghost stories. Assassinations stun time, radiating pain across borders and generations and the line between the living and the dead. Shakespeare filled his tragedies with denied lives that return at unpredictable times and in savage forms. His restless spirits can sometimes leave the stage to stalk the world, too.

To Hold the Mirror Up to Nature

The story of how Shakespeare changed our environment is both the craziest and most ordinary of stories. The most important events in our personal lives, and in human history, too, happen either by accident or by mistake, and nowhere is this terrible but comforting truth clearer than in the case of Shakespeare and the starlings in Central Park.

On March 6, 1890, a New York pharmaceutical manufacturer named Eugene Schieffelin brought natural disaster into the heart of the city completely without meaning to. Through the morning snow, which congealed at times to sleet, sixty starlings, imported at great expense from Europe, accompanied Schieffelin on the ride from his country house into Central Park—the noisy, dirty fulfillment of his plan to introduce every bird mentioned by Shakespeare into North America. Schieffelin loved Shakespeare and he loved birds. In 1858, he had introduced house sparrows into his New Jersey back garden and they had flourished, a supposed triumph gratifyingly commemorated in verse by William Cullen Bryant. The American Acclimatization Society, to which he belonged, had released other avian species found in Shakespeare—the nightingales and skylarks more commonly mentioned in his plays and poems—but none had survived. There was no reason to believe that starlings would fare any better. Schieffelin opened the cages and released the birds into the new world, without the smallest notion of what he was unleashing.

March 6, 1890, was bitterly cold, only twenty-three degrees, but I hope Schieffelin endured the weather long enough to enjoy his novelties. They must have looked so exotic against the snow, with their scintillating dark plumage spangled by yellow flecks, their odd, mechanistically jerky movements, their ruthlessly intelligent eyes. Today the things crowd the park, picking apart the garbage bags for rancid grapes and stale pizza crusts, collecting in intimidating numbers at dusk to squawk their ostentatious mating calls above the sounds of the streets. They have become a nightmarish pest, an ecological disaster of a kind all too familiar to our trampled world so altered by human carelessness, a world shaped by unintended consequences.

Schieffelin probably went home to a nice bath or a fire after his ceremony in the park. The starlings flew up to huddle under the eaves of the Museum of Natural History. Then they began to breed. They began to breed and they began to spread. From those initial sixty birds, and the forty Schieffelin released the following year, two hundred million starlings have filled North American skies. By 1895 small colonies had formed in New York City. Over the next hundred years, they extended their range from the Arctic regions of Canada to the tropics of Mexico, and the density of the birds continues to increase.

Why are they so successful? The protractor muscles of their beaks allow them to pry and to probe better than other birds. They can open their bills after pushing them into the soil, which allows them to forage for invertebrates easily and in drier areas. The starling's eyes have evolved to the narrow front of its face, giving it the perfect view for prying. Its binocular vision combined with its open-bill probing ability means that starlings can find insects in colder climates than other birds, which means that starlings do not have to migrate to warmer climates in winter, which means that they can take the best nesting holes during the breeding season. Which means that two hundred million starlings can spring from a hundred.

They are magnificent birds in themselves, wonderful mimics. Mozart discovered a starling in a Vienna store singing one of his better-known melodies, and took the avian fan home with him. We despise these birds for their success, which has wiped out entire cherry crops, ruined countless fields of winter-sown wheat, consumed masses of cattle feed. Their diseases are foul: avian tuberculosis and transmissible gastroenteritis for animals, histoplasmosis for humans. Ornithologists throughout the twentieth century watched with horror as starlings bullied bluebirds, Northern flickers, and woodpeckers out of their nests.

All their devastation sprung from one little speech in Shakespeare, and a forgettable speech at that. Shakespeare mentions starlings exactly once, in act 1, scene 3 of *Henry IV, Part One*. The king has ordered the roughneck hot-blooded soldier Hotspur never to mention the name of his brother-in-law Mortimer again, and Hotspur fantasizes about buying a starling for his lord just to have the thing repeat the name over and over.

> He said he would not ransom Mortimer,
> Forbade my tongue to speak of Mortimer,
> But I will find him where he lies asleep,
> And in his ear I'll holla "Mortimer!"
> Nay, I'll have a starling shall be taught to speak
> Nothing but "Mortimer," and give it him
> To keep his anger still in motion.
>
> (1.3.217–223)

Repetition is one of Shakespeare's favorite devices. He is constantly repeating characters' names and the most salient plot points of his stories, in part because he was writing for a rough theater crowd who needed to have the basic facts banged into their heads over and over again. The repetition of "Mortimer" in Hotspur's speech serves other purposes, however, mimicking the starling's own mimicry, and showing Hotspur in full rebellion, though at this point only linguistically. Unable to speak to the king's face, unable to emerge fully as a traitor, Hotspur loves the idea of the starling for its double status as both a gift and a curse, an object of beauty that is also a torment. In North America, the bird has turned out to be exactly that: a lovely monstrosity.

Within the span of a few decades, farmers and city planners were fighting back against the invasion. Almost immediately they began taking absurd measures. Here is a notice from the *New York Times* describing the anti-starling program of the citizens of Hartford, a program that combined rockets and Teddy bears:

Hartford, Conn., July 29, 1914.—Millions of noisy starlings, aided and abetted by a large number of bronze grackles, which for years offered a continuous problem to Bishop Nolan and the clergy of St. Joseph's Catholic Cathedral, in the spires of which they took squatters' rights, have settled in the tall trees of Washington Street, "the street of Governors," and one of the show spots of Hartford. So numerous and emphatic have become the complaints of the residents that Mayor Lawler turned the problem over to City Forester Muirhead and Lewis W. Ripley, President of the Bird Study Club. Today it was decided to try a combination of skyrockets and Teddy bears to scare the birds.

Teddy bears are to be fastened to the tree where the starlings have nested. Tonight a few rockets were fired through the trees, and if there is any noticeable result a fusillade will be discharged each evening for a week or more. The birds are out at dawn and keep up such a noise that no one in the neighborhood can sleep.

The attempt to contain starling damage in North America has tested the limits of human effort and ingenuity from the start. In 1921, a man hired to exterminate starlings from Poughkeepsie found the exertion required to shoot them so exhausting that he quit. In Washington, keeping starling-plagued national monuments clean produced elaborate technologies: The White House was fitted with speakers that buzzed owl calls; the Capitol was run with live wires around the columns where the starlings were congregating.

Refinements continue to this day. A recent issue of *Power* magazine, the trusted source of the power generation industry, endorsed the Bird-X Broadband Pro, a pest control speaker system that projects a combination of starling distress calls and the sounds of hawks and falcons with an effective range of ten thousand feet. In January 2009, the citizens of the Griggstown section of Franklin Township in New Jersey were startled by a sudden rain of starling corpses. A farmer in the area, under the guidance of the FDA, had put out poison to protect his cattle feed, and the birds, instead of dying quietly where they ate, decided to fly into town to die. Even in death, starlings manage to be wretchedly disgusting.

Eugene Schieffelin's obituary in the *New York Times* did not include any mention of the pretty birds through which he altered the face of a continent. Just the important stuff: that his father had been a prominent lawyer and that he had lived at 865 Madison Ave. His family had something of a wild history in the nineteenth century, with charges of bigamy, fortunes won and lost, capture and release by the Crow Indians. The whole world, Eugene included, must have felt that he had lived a life barely worth mentioning, working without distinction in the family business, indulging his eccentric passions for poetry and ornithology.

What would Shakespeare make of Schieffelin's surprisingly pernicious contribution? It may seem silly to ask four hundred years after the man stopped giving answers. But there, right at the end of *Henry IV, Part One*, the very play that conjured the starlings into the air, is a clue. Hotspur murmurs with his dying breath a message of cosmic humility:

> O Harry, thou hast robb'd me of my youth!
> I better brook the loss of brittle life
> Than those proud titles thou has won of me;
> They wound my thoughts worse than thy sword
>   my flesh:
> But thought's the slave of life, and life time's fool;
> And time, that takes survey of all the world,
> Must have a stop. O, I could prophesy,
> But that the earthy and cold hand of death
> Lies on my tongue: no, Percy, thou art dust,
> And food for—

(5.4.76–85)

Prince Hal, the man who has killed him, is the only one who can finish Hotspur's phrase: "For worms, brave Percy," he says, although he may be exhibiting the arrogance typical of the living. Why should Hotspur not be food for angels? The ellipsis shows just how thoroughly we lose control over the meaning of our lives the moment that we die.

In dying, Hotspur sees that he completely misunderstood the course of his life. He comes to understand that misunderstanding is fundamental to the human condition. Mortals cannot prophesy. We are time's fools. Even with the advantages of hindsight it's nearly impossible to tell how or why things turn out the way they do. If our younger incarnations were magically resurrected to examine our older selves, they would be overwhelmed by awe and disgust. If our ancestors woke up after a few decades of postmortem sleep, they would find us beyond their worst nightmares and their most outlandish fantasies. The most important life events are dates that almost didn't happen, parties almost forgotten about, books found on the street, trains caught at the last minute. This isn't airy philosophy. It's quotidian experience. The son everyone knows to be brilliant drops out to follow Phish. The daughter everyone thinks a bit slow grows up to be a pediatric oncologist. The future doesn't belong to us, no matter what we may dread or hope. Unpredictability is the very stuff of life.

The one feature that binds all the stories of all the characters in Shakespeare's plays together is that they never know what's about to wallop them. In *Love's Labour's Lost*, the young men swear they're going to lock themselves up to study. That's when the girls arrive. Macbeth comes to believe he's invincible. That's when death shows its naked face. Blindness to the future destroys Hotspur and Hamlet and Lear, it torments the kings of England and a horny thirteen-year-old girl sighing in Verona, upends the lives of nasty Jews and rapist Puritans, disturbs jolly old fat men and thin intellectual assassins, prostitutes and queens, pretentious carpenters and slumming princes. Seeing the future is no gift, as King Henry puts it in the second part of *Henry IV*:

> O God, that one might read the book of fate,
> And see the revolution of the times
> Make mountains level, and the continent,
> Weary of solid firmness, melt itself
> Into the sea, and other times to see

The beachy girdle of the ocean
Too wide for Neptune's hips; how chance's mocks
And changes fill the cup of alteration
With divers liquors! O, if this were seen,
The happiest youth, viewing the progress
    through,
What perils past, what crosses to ensue,
Would shut the book and sit him down and die.

                   (3.1.45–56)

Granted, this is the speech of a man who has betrayed his own king and who has been betrayed himself, and who cannot sleep for the demonic ironies that consume him, but his point has implications for all of us: Unpredictability may be one of life's greatest gifts.

Eugene Schieffelin was blind to the future he was creating, and Shakespeare was, too, for that matter, and so are we. The starlings in North America are two hundred million asterisks over the world and the gloss in the footnote is always the same: "We know nothing, we know nothing." Thought's the slave of life. The drop of ink Shakespeare quilled to write the word *starling* blotted out the sky of a continent he never visited.

At some point, Shakespeare's beauty entered Eugene Schieffelin's soul. How, we don't know. A few plays at school, no doubt, maybe an appearance in an amateur performance, the cocoon of private reading. A passion for Shakespeare bordering on insanity was hardly unique to Schieffelin in his time and place. He was living in New York during the anti-British Astor Place Riots in 1849, when competing Shakespeare performances led to bloody street fights. That night, the Englishman William Charles Macready dared to play Macbeth at the Astor Place Opera House while the American Edwin Forrest was performing the same role at the Broadway Theatre. Twenty people were killed and over one hundred fifty injured in the ensuing riots. Eugene Schieffelin loved Shakespeare and he loved birds. He wanted only to share the beauty he had known with the world at the large, and his evangelism took winged form. I'm sure I would have liked Schieffelin. I love Shakespeare and birds, too.

Whenever I see starlings, I try to see what Eugene Schieffelin saw on that bleak New York morning a hundred twenty years ago, a gorgeous, curious creature glimmering in its lovely purple and greens and shivering against the snow, knowing as little as we do.

Give Me My Robe, Put On My Crown

Shakespeare is simultaneously everywhere and nowhere in the world of politics. Four hundred years after his death, his speeches fit the shape of every mouth. Liberals can mumble through "now is the winter of our discontent," and conservatives can bluster off "the lady doth protest too much." Anyone with an interest in sounding grandiloquent can cull a telling phrase from one play or another. The greatest practitioner of the Shakespeare quote for political purposes in our times was the late senior Democratic senator from West Virginia, Robert Byrd, who repeatedly found obscure and beautiful lines from little-known plays such as *Henry VIII* or *King John*, and used them on perfectly apposite occasions. In 1994, he managed to quote once from every Shakespeare play on the floor of the Senate. This rare talent, though welcome, didn't mean that he was one of the great political thinkers of our time. (Then again, he was the longest-serving member of Congress in history.)

Oddly, Shakespeare's power is hardest to trace in the world of politics. It's so easy to find the precise confirmation of your own opinions and prejudices in Shakespeare that I hesitate to say he has any politics at all. He was harmless in his own time. After seeing *Richard II*, Queen Elizabeth I remarked, "I am Richard II, know ye not that?" That play came dangerously close to referring to the disastrous war in Ireland and the succession crisis. But if Queen Elizabeth had been genuinely worried about Shakespeare as a political force, she simply would have had him killed.

Knowing Shakespeare doesn't make you good, that's for sure. A few months after Hitler became chancellor, the Nazi Party issued a pamphlet entitled *Shakespeare—a Germanic Writer*, and in 1936, there were more productions of Shakespeare in Germany than in the rest of the world combined. Joseph Goebbels's favorite professor at Heidelberg was the Jewish Friedrich Gundolf, author of *Shakespeare and the German Spirit*. The Communists under Stalin elevated Shakespeare to the ranks of the "Great Thinkers of the Age," which culminated in Lenin and Stalin. During the Stalin era, over five million copies of Shakespeare were published in the twenty-eight languages of the Soviet Union, and thousands of productions of his plays were authorized. (Stalin, however, reportedly frowned on productions of *Hamlet*, disliking the prince's indecisiveness. Health-conscious theater directors avoided the Danish prince.)

Shakespeare doesn't make you bad, either. Even though Shakespeare served the nastiest totalitarian regimes of the twentieth century, he also became a tool for resistance against them. Hitler's Germany loved Shakespeare but also feared him. Ironically, the one play they couldn't handle was *The Merchant of Venice*, which languished after 1933. In 1938, *Merchant* was placed on the blacklist, to be confiscated from libraries. The Nazis and their ministry of propaganda feared two of the play's most salient features: Shylock's "Hath not a Jew eyes" speech (and since he has only five appearances in the entire play, it becomes complicated to cut any of his speeches) and his daughter Jessica's marriage to a non-Jew, which was illegal under Nazi law. One major production avoided this embarrassment by making Jessica a foster daughter rather than a blood relation, cutting Shylock's key line from the third act, "My own flesh and blood to rebel!" The ministry took no risks with that version. They hired actors to sit in the audience and shout insults at Shylock whenever he entered.

In Eastern bloc countries, over the second half of the twentieth century, Shakespeare grew more and more of a worry to the authorities. Polish critic Jan Kott's absurdist reading of the plays *Shakespeare Our Contemporary* was banned throughout the Communist world. After the Prague Spring in Czechoslovakia, productions of Shakespeare became a major avenue for protest. The Theatre on the Balustrade, in January 1969, put on a *Timon of Athens* rife with disillusionment and coded messages about the invading Soviets. They even added a rhyming couplet to the end of act 3, scene 1: "Those that have power to hurt and smother / Will heap one injury upon another." The cultural officials of the state caught on to these coded performances quickly enough and banned them. They couldn't stop everybody, though. In 1978, three dissident actors who had all been banned from performing in Czechoslovakia set up the Living-Room Theatre and put on *Macbeth* in the privacy of their own homes. Shakespeare became a way for actors without a stage to assert themselves.

Shakespeare serves many political masters but none of them faithfully, and ambivalence about the relationship between power and art riddles his plays. After Marc Antony's stirring funeral oration in *Julius Caesar*, the enraged crowd stumbles on Cinna the poet, whom they confuse with one of the conspirators, also named Cinna.

> THIRD PLEBEIAN: Your name, sir, truly.
>
> CINNA: Truly, my name is Cinna.
>
> FIRST PLEBEIAN: Tear him to pieces! He's a
> conspirator.
>
> CINNA: I am Cinna the poet, I am Cinna the
> poet.
>
> FOURTH PLEBEIAN: Tear him for his bad verses,
> tear him for his bad verses.
>
> CINNA: I am not Cinna the conspirator.
>
> FIRST PLEBEIAN: It is no matter, his name's
> Cinna; pluck but his name out of his heart,
> and turn him going.
>
> (3.3.26–34)

The crowd doesn't just kill Cinna. It rips him apart. Which is remarkable for two reasons. Ripping a poet apart is exceedingly violent and also nearly impossible to stage. Not only is the crowd mad in its rampaging violence; it is consciously mad, aware that it is slaughtering an innocent for no good reason. The pathetic excuses of the plebeians are even more horrifying than the violence they are trying to cover. The crowd is not just mistaken. The artist is, by an accident of language, its victim.

In *Julius Caesar*, art is a casualty of power, but in *Hamlet*, just the opposite: Art redeems history. The play-within-the-play is how the prince figures out whether to kill his uncle. A work of theater proves the justness of the assassination: "The play's the thing / Wherein I'll catch the conscience of the King." During the performance of *The Murder of Gonzago* in the play's third act, the murdering usurper Claudius calls for light, and Hamlet howls, "What, frighted with false fire?" For such a complicated play, the relationship between art and power is surprisingly simple. The play-within-a-play shows Claudius a direct representation of his own crime, and he cracks. All it takes is a clear representation of the cruelty of power to reveal what it is and what to do about it.

So Shakespeare gives us a double vision. Power rips art to pieces. And art reveals the hidden crimes of the powerful. Shakespeare predicted his own abuse and redemption. Just like Cinna in *Julius Caesar*, he was torn apart by Nazi and Communist mobs, and just like Hamlet and his uncle Claudius, his plays have offered false fire to startle the guilty heart of power everywhere.

So how are we to judge him? How are we to reckon up his effects on the world of power politics? After extensive public criticism of a performance of *The Merchant of Venice* at the Habimah Theater in Palestine in 1936, the theater responded by organizing a mock trial for Shakespeare just as Shakespeare had organized a trial for Shylock. The accused were William Shakespeare; the director Leopold Jessner, who had been a major force in Berlin's theatrical world before the Nazis came to power; and the Habimah Theater itself. Needless to say, in Israel, where any two people in an argument have three opinions, the prosecution and defense were both in shambles. Traditionalists argued that Shylock could not have been Jewish, because revenge was not a Jewish practice. The socialists argued that Shylock was a warning to the creeping spirit of speculation and profiteering starting to rear its head in the burgeoning state. In other words, Shylock was the wrong kind of Jew, not a Jew, or the ultimately wronged Jew all at the same time. *The Merchant of Venice* has been performed throughout Israel's history—after the founding of the state, after the conquests of 1967, after the beginnings of the intifada. In each case, it has provoked widespread outcry and defense.

Postwar Germany, as the only nation in the world that has honestly tried to confront its historical crimes, has also had a fraught relationship with *Merchant*. After an initial series of "expiation Shylocks" in which the character was played as an innocent, more sinned against than sinning, Germans began to incorporate their own recent past into the play. In a 1995 adaptation, the premise was Jewish prisoners at Buchenwald performing the play for their SS guards, after which all the actors were killed. A later German production incorporated scenes from *Merchant* into a concentration-camp narrative that converts the play's plot into scenes of Nazi torture. The moral simplicity of such outrage doesn't fit the complexities of history: The Nazi guards supposedly watching *The Merchant of Venice* for their amusement would, in reality, have been quite offended by the play. Despite the discomfort of the Israelis and the Germans, Shylock was too human for actual Nazis.

> I am a Jew. Hath not a Jew hands, organs, dimensions, sense, affections, passions? Fed with the same food, hurt with the same weapons, subject to the same diseases, healed by the same means, warmed and cooled by the same winter and summer as a Christian is?—if you prick us do we not bleed? If you tickle us do we not laugh? If you poison us do we not die? And if you wrong us shall we not revenge?
>
> (3.1.52–60)

Does it make this passage more brilliant or less that it comes out of the mouth of a stock Jewish villain? Shakespeare insists on the humanity even of people he stereotypes. That's the core of Shakespeare's politics. The twentieth century produced several extended experiments in the ways that men and women can be turned into objects to be processed or destroyed at will. Our common humanity is a massive embarrassment to such programs. Shakespeare insists on this embarrassment.

If, as George Orwell claimed, the future is a boot stamping on a human face over and over, Shakespeare has put human faces on display over and over in response. He insists above all on the fascination of each character, on each indestructible personhood. Or to put it another way: Like everyone else, like Hitler and Stalin and Churchill, I have found in Shakespeare the confirmation of my own political views—in my case an unremarkable but passionate brand of bland twenty-first-century humanism. Everybody finds what he or she is looking for, and I'm no exception.

Shakespeare is an indifferent political tool, glad to be of use. One might say: Shakespeare doesn't kill people, people kill people. Shakespeare doesn't free people, people free people. But Shakespeare was there at every front in the twentieth century, willing and able to betray all of his masters. He was there in Germany, in Czechoslovakia, in Russia, in Israel, happy to embarrass anyone with an ideology. Who has done better service? "The beauty of the world, the paragon of animals, the quintessence of dust," such is humanity, Hamlet says. Is it the least political statement ever made or the most important?

NOT MARBLE, NOR THE GILDED MONUMENTS

Shakespeare is the foremost poet in the world. All of the scriptwriting books cite him as the dominant influence on Hollywood. He has had more influence on the novel than any novelist. The greater the artist, the more he or she was influenced by Shakespeare. Dickens and Keats were more inspired by Shakespeare than anybody, and their familiarity with Shakespeare seems to have made them more original, not less. T. S. Eliot once said that the modern world is divided between the influences of Dante and Shakespeare, but that was mostly wishful thinking. Eliot, lover of categories, wanted the world to be neatly balanced between the pure, immaculately structured, Church-centered verse of Dante and the earthy, market-driven varieties of Shakespearean experience. Shakespeare won. More writers read him and imitate him than anybody else. He was, put simply, the first great writer of secular literature, and he has influenced all secular literature after him.

He is popular everywhere. Tonight you could go to see a Shakespeare performance in any major city in the world and most of the minor ones, on every continent. Shakespeare is an English writer only in the sense that soccer is an English sport. By the nineteenth century, he was the most widely performed playwright in both India and Japan. The most amazing aspect of Shakespeare's international success is how easy it's been. His power spreads seemingly of its own accord, even without institutional support, without imperial patronage or readers, with or without schools to plant his works in the soil of young minds. During the American Gold Rush, Shakespeare was wildly popular in the small towns along the frontier, his plays on par with prostitutes, booze, and poker as commodities of pleasure. When George and Mary Chapman, one of the most prominent acting families in the United States, opened the Jenny Lind Theater on November 20, 1851, in Nevada City, the locals were so delighted that they threw bags of gold dust on the stage after the show, and, finding the thud of the bags unsatisfying, followed it with rattling silver pieces—so much of it that the town suffered a shortage of silver money after the performance. When the Chapmans finally closed the show and moved on, four-fifths of the town's population escorted them to Sonora. The *Nevada City Nugget* described this response as "a tolerable success." Shakespearean actors made genuine fortunes in the Wild West. A leading man named James Murdoch earned $18,000 in the space of eight months, while the famous Baker family, who had made their careers in Boston, returned to the East $60,000 richer. In 1857, a San Francisco reporter described Shakespeare fatigue: "There is hardly a butcher or a newspaper boy in the city who does not understand 'like a book,' the majority of the playable plays of Shakespeare, so often have they seen them acted, ranted, or slaughtered upon our boards." He counted, in recent memory, eighty-six performances of *Hamlet*, sixty-three of *Richard III*, and fifty-seven of *Macbeth*. And that was in San Francisco alone.

Even in outer space, Shakespeare's the favorite. In *Star Trek VI: The Final Frontier*, the Klingon Chancellor

Gorkon quotes *Hamlet* at an intergalactic diplomatic function, adding, as an afterthought: "You have not experienced Shakespeare until you have read him in the original Klingon." Shakespeare has more passionate devotees outside England than in it; his influence has been, if anything, greater beyond the confines of those who can understand his language than within them. Gerhard Hauptmann, the great German playwright, wrote what so many of his countrymen have thought, that Shakespeare's birthplace was nothing more than an unfortunate accident: "If he was born and buried in England, it is in Germany that he truly lives." Foreigners' feelings of ownership over the Englishman are not merely a German phenomenon. In Bulgaria, the play *Romeo and Juliet* has infinitely more cultural importance than it does for any English-speaking nation; during the country's occupation by the Ottoman Empire, performances of *Romeo and Juliet* became overt statements of Bulgaria's connection to the Christian West rather than Muslim East. Politically speaking, *Romeo and Juliet* is more a Bulgarian play than an English one.

The malleability of his work to all places and times is supreme. Compare him to Dante and you see the contrast instantly. Dante matters less if you do not ascribe to a Catholic worldview, and he is vastly more beautiful in Italian than in translation. Shakespeare doesn't care what you believe. He's better in English, but he's willing to negotiate. Even after four hundred years, he remains an open trader in beautiful stories.

You can see the scope of his power even in the titles of other writers' work. *Infinite Jest*, by David Foster Wallace; *The Sound and the Fury*, by William Faulkner; *Brave New World*, by Aldous Huxley; *Pale Fire*, by Vladimir Nabokov. A thousand other novels begin with his words. "Why should anyone else attempt to write?" Virginia Woolf lamented in her diary. "Indeed I could say that Shakespeare surpasses literature altogether, if I knew what I meant." His overbearing influence on literature may be why I find it so delicious that Leo Tolstoy hated Shakespeare. Among so much sycophancy, it's refreshing to hear a lone dissenting voice. And not some weird nobody, either. I mean, it's Leo Tolstoy, the author of *Anna Karenina* and *War and Peace*.

Tolstoy and Anton Chekhov discussed Shakespeare frequently when they met on the Black Sea coast in the winter of 1901–1902, recuperating at the spas. Countess

Panina had given Tolstoy the run of her estate in Gaspra, six miles from Yalta. Their encounter took place in an atmosphere of the utmost luxury. Chekhov, obsessed about what clothes to wear to the first visit, was more like a nervous job applicant than the greatest short story writer of all time. He dismissed one pair of trousers for their foppish tightness, another for being too loutish and loose, and in the end arrived wearing an inoffensive dark suit and soft hat. Tolstoy greeted him in a rough peasant blouse and boots, which contrasted with the gorgeously furnished rooms. From the terrace they could peer over the delicate lawns through screens of oleander, cypress, and walnut, down to the sea. Tolstoy mostly talked and Chekhov listened. Tolstoy wasn't shy about complimenting or criticizing his junior. He adored the short stories, particularly "The Darling," which he described as "like lace made by a chaste young girl." (The compliment embarrassed Chekhov. "It's full of printer's errors," he replied.) But Tolstoy was equally unstinting in his contempt for Chekhov's plays. "Shakespeare wrote badly," he whispered into Chekhov's ear, "but you're worse still!"

The year after he delivered his magnificent backhander to Chekhov, Tolstoy sat down to write a whole book about

Shakespeare's failures as a writer. Even the best plays produced "an irresistible repulsion and tedium" in Tolstoy. His close examination of the complete works led him to a simple conclusion: "Shakespeare can not be recognized either as a great genius, or even as an average author." The current against which Tolstoy was swimming ran rugged and rapid, but he was not completely alone. George Bernard Shaw found Shakespeare's vision of life lacking in depth: "Shakespeare came out of his reflective period a vulgar pessimist, oppressed with a logical demonstration that life is not worth living." Socialists complained that he was not a socialist. The proper Edwardian critics tended to find him a tad grubby for their tastes. All of his haters were quick to cite earlier critics of Shakespeare, who were by no means small fry, including Ben Jonson and Voltaire among their ranks. But Tolstoy was special. He didn't restrict himself to a few jibes, a few cheap shots in periodical reviews. He spent a year rereading all of the plays, considering them deeply, and writing a spite-fueled evisceration of Shakespeare's reputation. *Tolstoy on Shakespeare* is one of the loneliest books I've ever read. It is magisterially unreserved and pure of heart.

It's as if everyone in the world loved the taste of strawberries and you wrote a book to prove, objectively, that strawberries don't taste good. "My disagreement with the established opinion about Shakespeare is not an accidental frame of mind," he writes. "Nor of a light-minded attitude toward the matter, but is the outcome of many years' repeated and insistent endeavors." Over the course of fifty years, he claims, he several times reread Shakespeare, in English and Russian and German, each effort only increasing his "indubitable conviction that the unquestionable glory of a great genius which Shakespeare enjoys . . . is a great evil, as is every untruth." In brief: Not only does he think your mother is ugly, he's tried to look at her year after year and from every possible angle, each time becoming only more convinced that not only is she ugly, it's evil that people might have ever called her beautiful.

Tolstoy on Shakespeare concentrates its contempt on *King Lear*, a play which most critics consider either the finest play in the canon or a play equaled only by *Hamlet* and which Tolstoy believes "does not satisfy the most elementary demands of art recognized by all." *King Lear* irritates Tolstoy. At first he can do little more than simply enumerate his irritations, each of which is crazier than the last. He believes, for example, that the play's action is "unnatural" and that the characters behave in arbitrary ways. "Lear has no necessity or motive for his abdication," he writes, which is factually incorrect. Lear wants to abdicate because he is worried that age will soon make him a weak king. This may not be the best motive for abdication, but it is still a motive. Characters in Shakespeare may not do things for the best reasons; they always do them for a reason.

Tolstoy also hates the play's anachronisms. *King Lear* is supposedly set in the ninth century A.D., and people did not speak like Shakespeare's Lear in ninth-century Britain, Tolstoy points out. But people in sixteenth-century England didn't speak like Shakespeare's Lear either. Shakespeare's language is an expressive medium rather than a strictly representational one. Tolstoy—the author of *War and Peace*!—seems unable or unwilling to comprehend this basic distinction between modes of writing. And then there's this: "In reading any of Shakespeare's dramas whatever, I was, from the very first, instantly convinced that he was lacking in the most important, if not the only means of portraying characters: individuality of language." I almost don't know what to say. To me, the "individuality of language" is exactly what makes Shakespeare Shakespeare. It's what distinguishes him, his plurality of voices, his variety of expression, the breadth of his ability to mimic and to penetrate convincingly into a seemingly endless array of perspectives. In *A Midsummer Night's Dream*, just to take the most obvious example, the royal couple speak in plain blank verse, the lovers speak in stichomythia (rhyming back and forth to one another), the lower classes speak in prose, and the fairies speak in a singsong meter akin to children's verse. *And that's one play*. No one produces characters with more individuality of language than Shakespeare. It is the single most outstanding feature of his work.

The most interesting question about *Tolstoy on Shakespeare* isn't literary but psychological: How did Shakespeare become Tolstoy's enemy? Despite what he claims in the introduction, a close reading of his journals reveals that Tolstoy did not read and reread Shakespeare regularly. His antipathy was clear as early as 1861, when Turgenev tried and failed to convince him of Shakespeare's merits. And as he aged, his prejudice hardened, as prejudices will do. So in 1884, he wrote to his wife that he found *Coriolanus* a nonsensical play "which only actors could like" (truly a damning insult). In 1894, he found *Julius Caesar* "amazingly foul." Throughout his life, he played a game with his fellow writers, who loved to hear him vent his infamous opinions on Shakespeare. Pick ten lines out of any play, he would say, and I'll tell you why they are so terrible and immoral. Much to his fury, he found that his colleagues were always so enraptured by whatever lines they had chosen, that they wouldn't listen to his arguments about their artistic failures. It is a testament to the force of Tolstoy's personality that this game never caused him to ask whether his own opinions needed changing.

Throughout his life Tolstoy collected examples of wild overenthusiasm, and at the end of *Tolstoy on Shakespeare* he just lays them out: "Shakespeare is the greatest moralist of all time"; "Shakespeare is the greatest genius that has hitherto existed"; "his only worthy rival was that same life which in his works he expressed to such perfection." It is possible to overpraise Shakespeare, and Tolstoy blames these excesses on the Germans (why not?) and "epidemic 'suggestion.'"

We can forgive Chekhov for not arguing against his elder at their meeting in Gaspra. It would be like arguing with your father about politics: What's the point? Who gains? No, Chekhov sat there and listened, savoring the conflict. "As bad as Shakespeare." The most ludicrous criticism ever received by a playwright, and yet it must have been somewhat devastating from the mouth of the world's greatest living prose writer. The exchange possessed exactly the kind of irony, fraught with ambiguous and shifting loyalties, that underlay Chekhov's best work.

Tolstoy would have been incapable of understanding such ambiguity. Most striking about his polemic is its rigidity. He doesn't offer the suggestion that Shakespeare is not to his taste; he abhors the existence of his plays. His concern is not a few deficiencies in technique; he damns the whole business. He doesn't wonder aloud whether Shakespeare may be overrated; he accuses Western culture of mass hypnosis. His attack focuses on three main points.

Shakespeare's bad technique. He finds the characters weak and spoiled. He finds the language overblown and exaggerated. Aesthetic categories are constantly being flouted. Where one is supposed to cry, one laughs. Where one is supposed to laugh, one breaks down weeping.

Shakespeare's amorality. The philosophy derived from his works amounts to this, according to Tolstoy: "Action at all costs, the absence of all ideals, moderation in everything, the conservation of the forms of life once established, and the end justifying the means." There is no trace of sympathy for the poor. He evidently failed to transcend conditions of the grubby, mercantile, provincial world of Renaissance English theater around 1600. He produced entertainment to numb the masses and to please the elites.

Shakespeare's lack of religion. For Tolstoy this absence was the fatal flaw and the main distinction of Shakespeare from earlier writers. "Art, especially dramatic art, demanding for its realization great preparations, outlays and labor, was always religious, i.e., its object was to stimulate in men a clearer conception of the relation of man to God."

Here's where we should pay attention: Shakespeare is a messy writer in which virtue and vice are fluid and no definite conclusions about God emerge. That is the core of Tolstoy's criticism. And he is absolutely correct. On a close examination of the plays, every part of his statement is true, and almost nobody in Tolstoy's time was willing to admit it.

Shakespeare is a messy writer. His verse combines the most extreme brilliance with sudden roughness, and he violates appropriate categories constantly. *Hamlet* is a tragedy, but nearly every scene is funny. Every second line from Hamlet is a joke. An entire group of Shakespeare's comedies—*All's Well That Ends Well*, *Measure for Measure*, *Troilus and Cressida*, *The Merchant of Venice*—have earned the title "problem comedies," because they are so dark, with such horrifying and vicious themes, that it seems ridiculous just to call them comedies. Then there's the incontestable fact that Shakespeare, while the highest of high poets, was also the most two-bit of hustlers. He cannot be contained in the dichotomy of saintly chaste artist against sinning prostituted entertainer. He is infuriatingly impure in all ways. His characters and his plots defy systems. Or as Tolstoy writes with disgust: "He teaches that morality, like politics, is a matter in which, owing to the complexity of circumstances and motives, one can not establish any principles." Macbeth's ambition drives him to murder and damnation, but Hamlet lacks enough of it. Lear is destroyed by the supposed virtue of renunciation. To the questions Is ambition good? Is renunciation good? Shakespeare answers firmly, "It depends." God's vagueness is another Tolstoy-maddening theme. Lear rails against the storm, but no divine figure emerges to save or to destroy him. Shakespeare fits at best uneasily into any religious viewpoint.

Chekhov thought that Tolstoy's main objection to other writers was that they weren't Tolstoyans, that they didn't follow his complete, coherent, and integrated philosophy of art, politics, and religion. To me, Tolstoy is like a crazed hermit who, digging through the mud for roots, throws aside nuggets of gold, which we may happily collect. He thought he had discovered the stupidity of Shakespeare and instead hit exactly the key to his enormous appeal: Shakespeare is a messy writer with a complex view of morality whose conception of the universe is a bottomless, shifting ground. That's exactly why he is the dominant writer of our era. It's a side effect that, because he lacks clear expression, good ideas, and depth of purpose, he therefore failed to fit the working definition of a great artist in Tolstoy's time. "Shakespeare might have been whatever you like, but he was not an artist," Tolstoy said, again correctly. On the terms by which the critics of his day, both the big lights such as Carlyle and Ruskin as well as the main body of literary opinion, Shakespeare *should have been* a bad writer. Tolstoy just believed his aesthetic philosophy more than the world's taste. The question isn't why Tolstoy was so crazy but why he was so alone.

The reason we love such a messy writer, with a contingent sense of right and wrong and a vague attitude toward the ultimate meaning of the universe, is that we are messy, and the ultimate meaning of right and wrong is contingent, and our sense of the universe is vague. "It depends" is the accurate answer to most questions. It might not be the answer we prefer. Tolstoy objected to the messiness of Shakespeare's means and purposes. Shakespeare violates the idea that life can be fully understood. And if life cannot be understood, then absolute justice is a permanent dream never to be realized, and art does not serve the world but serves itself. Tolstoy saw the subversive potential: If Shakespeare is a great artist, then the world, at bottom, is gorgeous and muddy and ultimately impenetrable. And then Tolstoy would be gorgeous and muddy and ultimately impenetrable.

The meeting between Chekhov and Tolstoy was a

mille-feuille of contrasts; Chekhov from the middle class dressing up in his best clothes against Tolstoy the aristocrat in affected peasant's garb; Chekhov the silent listener against Tolstoy the rambler; the miniaturist against the master of the sweeping epic. But the basic conflict, the most fundamental difference between the two men, was that Tolstoy believed that things could be understood, and Chekhov did not. Put another way: Tolstoy believed that life should be fair, and Chekhov didn't think it could be. Put yet another way: Chekhov understood Shakespeare and Tolstoy did not.

Shakespeare recognizes the messiness of life as does no other writer, but it comes at a cost of an easy understanding of life's ultimate purpose. More than anything, Tolstoy couldn't stand Shakespeare's complicated endings. Which is why he preferred the original *King Leir* chronicle play to Shakespeare's version. To me, this preference for *King Leir* is baffling. It is quite one thing to dislike Shakespeare. I suppose that's fair enough. If you don't like strawberries, you don't like strawberries. It's something else entirely to say you like *King Leir.* That's like saying you like the taste of drywall. Don't get me wrong. I dearly love the weird world of all English Renaissance drama, not just Shakespeare; it's the kind of love that makes me tell strangers they should read *'Tis Pity She's a Whore*, a positive incest love story, or *The Spanish Tragedy*, in which Revenge comes from hell to watch over the action. English Renaissance drama is raw and sophisticated, strangely primitive but also completely modern. Revengers sweep aside curtains to reveal skeletons. Dukes rape corpses. Women dressed as men fall in love with each other as men. Bodies start bleeding in the presence of murderers. A man bites off his own tongue so that he will be unable to talk under torture. *King Leir*, however, is not among the number of these bizarre and wonderful dramas; it is mediocre beyond belief. No one would ever read it if it were not for its status as raw material for Shakespeare. For Tolstoy, "the whole of this old drama is incomparably and in every respect superior to Shakespeare's adaptation."

The principal difference between *King Leir* and *King Lear*, other than the fact that one is as limp as soggy bread and the other is strong, is that *King Leir* has a happy ending. Cordelia reconciles with her father. The King of the Gauls overthrows the wicked husbands of the bad sisters. Justice is served, and the comforting assertion that life is fair and makes sense is reiterated. Not in Shakespeare. Justice, in *King Lear*, is a twisted grotesquerie. In act 5, scene 3, as Lear and Cordelia are led off in defeat, the terrible ending is full of joy. The king dances into captivity:

> Come, let's away to prison;
> We two alone will sing like birds i'th'cage:
> When thou dost ask me blessing, I'll kneel down,
> And ask of thee forgiveness: so we'll live,
> And pray, and sing, and tell old tales, and laugh
> At gilded butterflies, and hear poor rogues
> Talk of court news; and we'll talk with them too,
> Who loses and who wins; who's in, who's out;
> And take upon 's the mystery of things,
> As if we were Gods' spies.

(5.3.8–17)

Lear finds his saintliness in a true abdication, a willful refusal of responsibility, a flight from the world. Old tales are nearly as good as fresh ones. Life is pretty butterflies. Politics is amusing "court news." Physical enslavement has become spiritual liberation. Is it a happy conclusion? It depends.

At the very end of the play, after Cordelia has died, Lear is offered a return to the full majesty of his glory, a return to the way things once were. The Duke of Albany, who has conquered the forces of Lear's evil daughters, declares: "All friends shall taste / The wages of their virtue, and all foes / The cup of their deservings." Yet justice is not enough for Lear. Even if life were fair, it would not be fair:

> Never, never, never, never, never!
> Pray you, undo this button: thank you, Sir.
> Do you see this? Look on her, look, her lips,
> Look there, look there!
>
> (5.3.307–310)

What is he seeing there? Breath? Does he die believing that she is alive? Or does he instead see the perfect O of her rounded lips, the cipher of meaning rather than any definite meaning? Does he die in the fullness of hope or a haunted terror of nothingness? It depends.

I have seen, with my own eyes, a theater full of adolescents, removed from Shakespeare by four centuries and a continent, weep at this final scene. After experiencing *King Lear*, the concept of justice seems like a ludicrous practical joke our ancestors played on us out of spite. Even if life were fair, who could stand the terms? Tolstoy desired life to be fair so much that he ended up convincing himself that life is fair. No wonder *King Lear* infuriated him.

Tolstoy and Chekhov, after their final meeting in Gaspra on March 31, 1902, never saw one another again. Tolstoy sat down to write his polemic against Shakespeare, and two years later Chekhov was dead. Their deaths show the difference *King Lear* can make in your life. Tolstoy, who found the plot line of the play so unbearably unnatural, ended pursued by the demons of a deep sense of betrayal across the Russian steppe with his single faithful daughter by his side, to die in a cabin in a strange village. George Orwell called it "a phantom reminiscence of *Lear*." Chekhov died in a kind of inversion of tragedy. Though he was delirious from fever, he managed to remain calm. "Everything's useless now," he told the doctor, who was sending out for oxygen. "I'll be a corpse before it gets here." So they ordered champagne, and drank it off slowly. "It's a long time since I've had champagne," were his final words. No writer, not even

Tolstoy, can escape Shakespeare's influence entirely. He's just too lifelike to ignore. He's too messy, too full, too vague, too complicated. You find Shakespeare even in the books of people who despise him. Tolstoy, unable to understand *Lear*, repeated his tragedy. Chekhov, who understood *Lear* perfectly, toasted life instead.

A King of
Infinite Space

What if Shakespeare had never lived? What if he, like so many children of the sixteenth century, had died in childhood, just another lost infant son of an unknown Stratford glove maker? Instead of the bland monument with its threatening inscription—"cursed be he who moves my bones"—imagine a nameless grave, a corpse knocked about and forgotten long ago in the Warwickshire muck. How would the world be different without him?

Most writers spend their lives avoiding the question of what writing amounts to. It's an annoying question and tends to be asked by annoying people, like your parents and their friends and the businessmen at gala fundraisers. I've never yet heard a satisfying answer, because no matter what anyone says, there's almost always a better way to achieve the intended goal than by writing. If you want to improve the world, go plant a tree in the desert or chain yourself to a whaling vessel or sign up to teach underprivileged kids in an at-risk neighborhood. Samuel Johnson, the eighteenth-century critic and wit, famously said that anyone who doesn't write for money is a blockhead, but sadly the opposite is true. If you want money, may I suggest corporate law? Or at least aluminum siding.

In this book, I've tried to give real, solid, material answers to the question of what Shakespeare changed: starlings, psychotherapy, the conceptualization of adolescence and race, the modern English lexicon, Lincoln's corpse, specific books. But all these global effects are accidental by-products of Shakespeare's power to move individuals—they are the material echoes of his profound and mysterious presence in the lives of distant readers and audiences.

Shakespeare belongs to anyone who wants to tell his stories, no matter how remote. There's a famous anecdote, beloved by Shakespeare professors, about an anthropologist named Laura Bohannan who went to study the Tiv tribe in a remote corner of the Nigerian interior during the early sixties. It was the rainy season in Benue, when the Tiv can't work and can't perform the rituals that anthropologists such as Professor Bohannan study. Instead, the Tiv start drinking in the morning and they tell stories all day. Eventually they asked Bohannan for a story, and it just so happened that she had a copy of *Hamlet* with her. She decided to give it a try.

The questions began immediately, from the first scene. The Tiv could not understand why the ghost would come for Hamlet. It wouldn't be the duty of a son to avenge his father, but the duty of his father's brothers. They also heartily approved of Claudius's marriage to Gertrude, which is a problem if you want the play to make sense. An old man commented to his companions: "I told you that if we knew more about Europeans, we would find they were really very like us. In our country also, the younger brother marries the elder brother's widow and becomes the father of his children." It took the anthropologist several attempts to untangle this knot of contention, but the whole play required a separate Tiv explanation. When Hamlet confronts his mother, the audience erupted in "shocked murmurs." How could a son scold his mother? Hamlet, as written, was all too unbe-lievable. So the Tiv insisted on straightening it out for the anthropologist. Once they had corrected the play, though—explaining the chains of magic and revenge that fit the Tiv worldview—they enjoyed it. "Sometime you must tell us some more stories of your country," one of the old men told Bohannan. "We, who are elders, will instruct you in their true meaning, so that when you return to your own land your elders will see that you have not been sitting in the bush, but among those who know things and who have taught you wisdom."

Everyone makes his or her own *Hamlet*, and I make my own, too. I like to read Shakespeare in mall food courts. As long as the seats are not too uncomfortable, a mall food court is one of the best places to read and write. I don't know why. Maybe it's because it caters to our shallowest desires, and shallowness is deeply re-laxing. Everything is slick and consumable. Teams of teenage boys scope video games and girls. Old guys read the paper, nursing fast-food coffees. It's all so calm, the opposite of the rowdy theaters where the plays were orig-inally performed. Has there ever been a more satisfying afternoon in human history than eating a Big Mac after buying chinos at the Gap? Literature matters more than ever in these conditions, as a bulwark against the tidal smoothness of modernity, the plastic waves that threaten to overwhelm us and fatten us and stupefy us. In a mall food court, the power and the glory of a play like *Hamlet* shine out.

Been in a mall food court recently? Notice how many skulls there are? Teenagers wear them on their Vans. I've seen them in crystal patterns on baseball caps and on the hoods of hoodies. In the gossip magazines, Gwyneth Paltrow pushes her babies around with skulls on her scarves. At the shoe store, my son, when he was three, wanted sneakers that flash up and down when you jump, and then when I brought them home, I found that they were covered with hundreds of small skulls. In our time, the skull serves the same iconic purpose that the peace symbol once did, to establish that the wearer is in touch with the current of present reality.

By the time Shakespeare put the skulls in *Hamlet*, they already had a long tradition in Western Europe. The memento mori—the reminder of death—took many distinct forms. The simplest would be a small skull bead at the end of a rosary. In Holland and Germany, some of these beads, in the shape of a skull, would fold open to display scenes of the apocalypse and resurrection. More elaborate reminders of death developed over the centuries. Maybe the most elaborate was the crypt of the Capuchin monks in Rome. Piles of skulls in a dozen rooms shaped into fireplaces or shelves, the shoulder bones making delirious patterns on the ceiling. A sign reads: "We are as you once were. You will be as we are." Before Shakespeare, the point of the skull was to remind us of our ultimate end, to make us see beyond the superficialities of the material world we inhabit, to keep our gaze firmly focused on death.

In *Hamlet*, Shakespeare turns this icon of mortality into the skull of a jester. The scene with Yorick's skull may be the most famous scene in all of Shakespeare, maybe the most famous scene in theater altogether. Scholars call it comic relief because the gravediggers joke around as they toss up the bones from the crowded soil. I have always found the term *comic relief* inappropriate when applied to the gravedigger scene. Not because the scene isn't funny. It is. But all the scenes in *Hamlet* are funny. The sadness is comic, and the humor is anguished; the two are not separate. One does not relieve the other.

HAMLET: Alas, poor Yorick. I knew him, Horatio, a fellow of infinite jest, of most excellent fancy. He hath borne me on his back
a thousand times. And now how abhorred
in my imagination it is! My gorge rises at
it. Here hung those lips that I have kissed
I know not how oft. Where be your gibes
now, your gambols, your songs, your flashes
of merriment that were wont to set the table
on a roar? No one now to mock your own
grinning? Quite chop-fallen? Now get you
to my lady's chamber and tell her, let her
paint an inch thick, to this favour she must
come. Make her laugh at that.

(5.1.178–189)

So far, so unremarkable, a speech firmly in the established tradition, the mockery that death makes of our
daily, inconsiderate lives, asking the question of what lies
beyond what we see and what we know. A kind of nihil-
istic jesting.

Then the play takes a strange turn, an unprecedented
turn even:

HAMLET: To what base uses we may return,
    Horatio. Why, may not imagination trace
    the noble dust of Alexander till he find it
    stopping a bung-hole?

HORATIO: 'Twere to consider too curiously to
    consider so.

HAMLET: No, faith, not a jot; but to follow
    him thither with modesty enough, and
    likelihood to lead it. As thus: Alexander
    died, Alexander was buried, Alexander
    returneth into dust. The dust is earth, of
    earth we make loam, and why of that loam
    whereto he was converted might they not
    stop a beer-barrel?

Imperious Caesar, dead and turned to clay,
Might stop a hole to keep the wind away.
O, that that earth, which kept the world in awe,
Should patch a wall t'expel the winter's flaw.

                                    (5.1.196–209)

Hamlet reverses the usual spiritual practice of the memento mori; instead of the skull's making him less mate-

rialistic, it makes him more so; it shows us that even gods among men such as Alexander and Caesar are just mud. He uses the skull as a symbol of the shallowness of even the most profound human matters. He makes a mockery of making a mockery of the pointlessness of human concerns. He uses the device of religion to arrive at the basest kind of crudity.

There's only one passage of Shakespeare criticism that I think about as often as I think about Shakespeare. It comes from the Oxford scholar A. C. Bradley's *Shakespearean Tragedy* (1904), much out of fashion today, but, I believe, better written than any other piece of criticism about Shakespeare in the century that has followed. I am going to quote a passage at some length because I think it is so, so beautiful.

> This central feeling [of Shakespearean tragedy] is the impression of waste. With Shakespeare, at any rate, the pity and fear which are stirred by the tragic story seem to unite with, and even to merge in, a profound sense of sadness and mystery, which is due to this impression of waste. "What a piece of work is man," we cry; "so much more beautiful and so

much more terrible than we knew! Why should he be so if this beauty and greatness only tortures itself and throws itself away?" We seem to have before us a type of the mystery of the whole world, the tragic fact which extends far beyond the limits of tragedy. Everywhere from the crushed rocks beneath our feet to the soul of man, we see power, intelligence, life and glory, which astound us and seem to call for our worship. And everywhere we see them perishing, devouring one another with dreadful pain, as though they came into being for no other end.

Hamlet doesn't just think about death or obsess about his own mortality. He is not at all the morbid type, a proto-vampire, a goth *avant le lettre*. He looks at Yorick's skull and sees two separate truths, neither of which he can escape. Death casts a pall over the feast of life and death nourishes life. Does the skull mean we should abstain from the pleasure of the flesh? Or rather should the lesson of the skull be Eat, drink, and make merry, for tomorrow we shall die? Hamlet is melancholy and jokey at the same time because he feels both these contradictory truths simultaneously.

The skulls in the food court at the mall have the same two-faced glamour. They adorn the everyday objects of urban and suburban America to give a pretense of depth, spreading a radiant materialism, a daring superficiality that recognizes death but nonetheless wants a new iPhone and Prada sunglasses and blue jeans in the latest style. Look around an Urban Outfitters: Shakespeare is current up to the second. He means *now*. Hamlet in the graveyard scene arrives at the decadent materialism of the mall, the flouting of the authenticity of death. Hamlet's father haunts the ancient battlements of Elsinore. Hamlet haunts the food court.

I can almost see him as he stalks the mall, pausing to analyze the teenage girls' discussions of the advantages and disadvantages of their phones, commenting acerbically on the movies showing at the multiplex, wondering aloud at the perfect appropriateness of a store named The Gap. There is providence in the fall of a French fry onto the bleached floor.

Shakespeare makes the world shiver. He makes everyday things vibrate in their preciousness and transience. This personal, private shiver is the source of all his worldliness—his public power, which extends, as we've seen, from the birds in the sky to the words in our mouths, from brands of Cuban cigars to what you did in bed last night, from Lincoln to Obama. The ripples of Shakespeare stretch further and further, on and on, to the limit of the world, because the stone of his meaning sinks and sinks without ever touching the bottom of our selves.

To Be or Not to Be

Any one of the previous ten chapters in this book is enough to argue that Shakespeare is the world's most powerful writer. More: Any chapter of this book is enough to show that he was one of the most powerful figures in world history generally. No other writer is so widely disseminated. No other writer has shaped sex or adolescence or language or racial understanding or literature as much as Shakespeare. This vast power, the stupendous size and scope of his influence, makes the question of Shakespeare's identity all the more vital and fascinating than it would be if he were merely a beloved poet. About Shakespeare, we need to know: Who is this man whose words have changed the world? Shakespeare is everywhere but who is Shakespeare?

Unfortunately, the question is nearly impossible to answer. We know amazingly little about the man who spread everywhere. Even basic facts are obscure. Take his birthday. Most biographies will tell you that Shakespeare was born on April 23, 1564, but there's no record of his actual date of birth. The Stratford church recorded his christening on April 26, and everyone accepts April 23 as his birthday because the nineteenth-century biographer Sidney Lee in his classic *Life of William Shakespeare* assumed that the common practice in the period was for baptism to follow birth by three days. But there's no three-day rule in *The Book of Common Prayer*; other birth and christening records from the period show a generally loose attitude to the timing of the event. Baptism could be a day later, could be a week later. So why did Sidney Lee select April 23? Shakespeare died on April 23, 1616. April 23 is also, neatly, the day of St. George, England's patron saint. Absent solid facts, neatness prevails.

We don't know when Shakespeare was born, and we don't know how old he was when he died. We don't even know how to pronounce his name. He left only six signatures behind, and they're inconsistent with each other. Even though there was no set authoritative and correct orthography in the period, most people had a way they liked to write their own name and stuck to it. Not Shakespeare. (Or is that Shakespere or Shakspear?)

There are a few, slippery details that we can more or less claim to know. At the age of eighteen, Shakespeare married Anne Hathaway, a woman supposedly seven years his elder, who was pregnant at the time. Other writers love this juicy tidbit. The age gap between William and Anne is the basis of the interpretation of *Hamlet* in James Joyce's *Ulysses* and the plot of Anthony Burgess's novel *Nothing Like the Sun*. Scholars sometimes use the story to spice up bland interpretations. They see Shakespeare's youthful sexual education by the more experienced older woman behind the Arden Wood sexual antics in *As You Like It*. The difficult marriages in *The Winter's Tale* or *Taming of the Shrew* must be fictionalized versions of his own marriage, begun in unwilling entrapment by a woman on the edge of becoming unmarriageable. I almost hate to be the one to point out that all these fantasies are based on a single piece of evidence. A scrap. Anne's gravestone, carved in 1623, reads "Being of the age of 67 Yeares." By no means were the gravestones in this period reliable. It is entirely possible that the *67* should be *61*, which would mean that Shakespeare and Anne were roughly the same age, and all of the scholars and all of the novelists have dreamed up a completely incorrect Shakespeare, with a marriage that never existed. The entire biographical edifice might well have been built on a typo. The historical record of early modern England is full of typos. There's even a second notice of Shakespeare's marriage, in Worcester, in which he's marrying an Anne Whately, not an Anne Hathaway. The discrepancy has led to an explosion of fanciful theories—was there another, younger Anne? Was Shakespeare faced with a choice between a young Anne and an old Anne, between love and duty? Or did the clerk just screw up?

Shakespeare's life was strewn with legal documents that tantalize and disappoint. The reverend Joseph Green, the scholar who transcribed Shakespeare's will in 1747, was overwhelmed by the insignificance of the find: "The Legacies and Bequests therein are undoubtedly as he intended; but the manner of introducing them, appears to me so dull and irregular, so absolutely void of ye least particle of that Spirit which Animated Our great Poet; that it must lessen his Character as a Writer, to imagine ye least Sentence of it his production." He left his daughter

Judith a nice silver bowl. Can you really bring yourself to care? Famously he left his "second-best bed" to his wife, which does seem strange. What does it mean, though? Is it a postmortem sexual insult, a final jab at his older wife (if she was indeed older)? Or is it the opposite, a gesture of tenderness? Often the best bed in rural homes was reserved for guests. Was the second-best bed the one that Shakespeare and Anne slept in, the bed filled with matrimonial memories? Or does it mean nothing?

Shakespearean biography is a noble but necessarily futile endeavor. How would you feel if a scholar in the future tried to write your biography on the basis of your birth certificate, your will, and a handful of parking tickets? The best biographers, such as the American scholar Samuel Schoenbaum, the ones who stay within the realm of demonstrable reality, flesh out their bare-bones Shakespeares with "portraits of the age," trying to describe "the typical schoolhouse," "the world of Shakespeare's theater," "the streets of London during the reign of Elizabeth," and so on. Even this necessarily limited and fastidious approach to the historical record has the danger of slipping into the realm of fiction, especially when the plays are taken as evidence for Shakespeare's view of the world around him. We know that he attended the King's New School in Stratford-upon-Avon, for example. We know that Romeo says "Love goes toward love, as school-boys from their books." We know that Jaques in *As You Like It* describes

> . . . the whining school-boy, with his satchel
> And shining morning face, creeping like snail
> Unwillingly to school.
>
> (2.7.145–147)

There are other mentions of unhappy schoolboys in *Henry VI, Part 2* and *Much Ado About Nothing* as well. And so most biographers assume he hated school. And yet he read everything. Everything. He certainly learned his Ovid at King's New School and used it throughout his career.

More to the point: Who lives typically? Who attends a typical school? Everybody's experience is extraordinary, and surely that must be doubly true for Shakespeare, the most original mind of his time. We do not know Shakespeare and we probably never will. Generations of scholars have so far uncovered only the blandest and least insightful of details. The man who thrust his work everywhere into the world has left no meaningful trace of himself behind.

The absence of biographical detail has left a huge chasm to fill. As soon as Shakespeare's body was in the ground, fascinating, dubious legends sprang up about him. Some of these are good fun. He probably did not have a best friend who was equally brilliant but died in childhood, depriving the world of another genius. But it's amusing to think so. It's amusing to picture Shakespeare as a butcher's boy, who, in John Aubrey's retelling in *Brief Lives* "when he killed a calf, he would do it in a high style, and make a speech." Unfortunately, Shakespeare's father was a glover and not a butcher. Glovers didn't slaughter their own animals.

The legends of Shakespeare's childhood in Stratford have a tendency to lessen him, as if, to process the magnitude of the local boy's talent, the villagers had to diminish the man, to make him more human, one of their own. Nicholas Rowe, a seventeenth-century antiquarian who compiled a collection of local Stratford anecdotes, tells the story of young Shakespeare running with a pack of village toughs caught poaching deer on the property of the local justice of the peace, Sir Thomas Lucy of Cherlecot. After being whipped and imprisoned, so the story goes, Shakespeare composed a nasty ballad about Sir Thomas, which infuriated the bigwig so successfully that Shakespeare had to flee Stratford for London and, incidentally, a brilliant theatrical career. Another Stratford legend portrays Shakespeare as a drunken loser during the years of his retirement from the theater. He had heard that the townsfolk in the adjacent town of Bidford considered themselves champion drinkers, and led a Stratford contingent there to challenge them. Told that the serious drinkers had gone to the Evesham Fair, Shakespeare challenged the lesser Bidford drinkers, the "sippers," to a battle which he nonetheless managed to lose. Unable to walk back to Stratford, he tumbled unconscious under a nearby crabtree. This crabtree became legendary in Bidford as the place where Shakespeare slept off his big drunk. Souvenir seekers soon tore it to shreds.

Shakespeare fans will do anything for a piece of him. They'll make up silly stories. They'll rip down strangers' trees. Any town in the world called Stratford—you can bet on it—will have a souvenir shop, equipped with keychains that bleat famous phrases when you push a button, mugs bearing the ugly etching from the First Folio, finger puppets of his major characters, sweatshirts, fridge magnets, and Shakespeare action figures. In 1759, when the Reverend Francis Gastrell bought Shakespeare's house in Stratford-upon-Avon, he grew so tired of strangers taking cuttings from the mulberry tree outside his window that he had the whole thing cut down and sold to a company in Birmingham. The Birmingham woodworkers conveniently found that mulberry tree to be amazingly giving; they were able to make more furniture from that one tree than from any other tree in history except, maybe, the True Cross.

The desire for a glimmer of Shakespeare's personality naturally attracts frauds and scams, the way a messy kitchen naturally attracts mice. In the nineteenth century, criminal organizations flourished at the business of making fake portraits of Shakespeare. The process was simple enough. Take any half-decent, or even lousy, portrait from the Jacobean period, carve a date and Shakespeare's name at the bottom (sometimes misspelled for the illusion of accuracy) and then pass it on. The market was insatiable, never ending. And the suckers wanted to believe the lies, that was the beautiful part. One creative forger took to buying family portraits from the period and cutting them up to make several different Shakespeares at a time. Even in the business of Shakespeare portrait forgery, economies of scale are everything.

Shakespearean portraiture, like Shakespearean biography, seems designed to flout certainty. The only image of Shakespeare possibly taken during his lifetime was the Flower portrait, though even it may be a fancified copy of the etching in the First Folio, which was definitely posthumous.

Could there be a less revealing, less satisfying portrait of the man? There are police-artist sketches that tell us more about their subjects. It doesn't even look like a face, much less like the face of the "spirit of his age." The head is a spherical void. The eyes stare stupidly behind a perspective-experiment nose and brow, transfixed and cold, lacking feeling or judgment.

The Chandos portrait, the first acquisition of the National Portrait Gallery in London, looks, at least to me, a little more like the author of *Titus Andronicus* and *Hamlet* and *The Tempest*.

The Flower portrait.

The Chandos portrait.

Here we have a warm sensualist, capable of daring (with his sharp gold earring), a man clearly connected to the tradition of European humanism, or at least somebody who knew enough to find a decent painter. Unfortunately we don't really know whether the Chandos portrait is Shakespeare. It could be just some random guy with a similar bald-mullet hairstyle and intelligent eyes. The Duke of Chandos acquired the painting in 1747, along with the story that Sir William Davenant, who claimed to be Shakespeare's godson, once owned the thing. The key word is *claimed*. The Chandos could be. Or not.

Then there's the Sanders portrait.

The painting was discovered in an attic in Canada a decade ago, a strange place for Shakespeare to wind up, but as I'm writing this book in a Canadian attic, I'd like to imagine that it's not impossible. After an immense battery of tests from experts on two continents, there's no proof that the Sanders portrait *isn't* Shakespeare. The image was painted in the correct period and place. It may lack the stately calm and grandeur of the Chandos portrait, but the subject has some Shakespearean qualities, at least to my eye: He's mischievous, sprightly, energetic to the point of bursting, funny, intelligent, removed, secre-

The Sanders portrait.

tive. And balding. I find the Sanders portrait the most tempting to believe in. When I close my eyes and see Shakespeare propped up in a corner of some Elizabethan tavern working through the dialogue between Richard III and Anne in his head while eavesdropping on a conversation about rumors at court, he looks like the fellow in the Sanders portrait. But I know that the Sanders-portrait fellow is, most likely, somebody else. Somebody who, while no doubt a fun guy and worth drinking with, did not write *Romeo and Juliet* and *A Midsummer Night's Dream* and *Coriolanus*.

History has not given us Shakespeare's face, which may be for the best. Shakespeare himself had no faith in faces. "God has given you one face and you make yourself another," Hamlet tells his mother. Innocent Desdemona protests: "I have no judgment in an honest face." The soon-to-be murdered King Duncan in *Macbeth* complains: "There's no art to find the mind's construction in the face." If we want Shakespeare, we're not going to find him in his face. We certainly aren't going to find him in any of his portraits.

If we're going to find him, it's going to be in the plays. Nobody ever left behind a richer or more complete record of thought on every conceivable subject and situation. And yet their very strength as plays limits how much they can tell us about their author. Shakespeare manages to inhabit his characters so perfectly that they leave little trace of himself in their language. He could be anyone in words. His old woman is as convincing as his young man. His murderer is as living as his saint, his thin assassin as precise as his jolly nurse. He realizes the fantasy of a fairy world with the same ease as he manages the hard-hearted realism of the Eastcheap brothels. The language is so acrobatic and so varied that establishing consistency is nearly impossible. His plays are sublime mysteries. They point at the world, and Shakespeare himself huddles behind his mirror.

Then there's the seemingly minor but vital point that we have no idea which version of his plays Shakespeare intended us to read. Just as his biography is incomplete, just as his portraits don't give us his real face, the texts of his plays are unstable and unreliable and maddeningly incomplete. Almost every play you read in high school or have seen onstage is a conflation, meaning that editors and directors take the multiple versions of the plays' texts as they originally appeared and smush them together, tucking away the hundreds and thousands of minor decisions they have to make to create a play that normal people (as opposed to professional scholars) can stand to read or see.

The problem is that Shakespeare didn't leave manuscripts or authorized versions. What we possess of his work is either the product of various fly-by-night publishers who printed, without Shakespeare's consent or involvement, small quarto editions of his plays, or the version his friends Heminge and Condell published posthumously, a Collected Edition called the First Folio, in 1623. Because most of the plays exist in multiple versions, none of which have an absolute claim to authority, almost every Shakespeare work is a scholarly quagmire.

Even the specific words Shakespeare meant to use are often impossible to establish, for instances, the line from Othello's final speech when he asks his fellow Venetians to speak,

> Of one whose hand,
> Like the base Indian, threw a pearl away
> Richer than all his tribe.

You could interpret the line this way: The reference to the Indian is a brilliant evocation of the Spanish crimes in the New World which were just beginning to capture the popular imagination in England (even the name of Iago, Othello's nemesis, is an allusion to Spain's patron saint, Saint Iago the Moorslayer). The passage is then a subtle nod to the nascent racism of the transatlantic economy. Which is all very well and good, except that the Indian appears only in the Quarto edition of *Othello*. In the Folio, the same line reads,

> Of one whose hand
> Like the base Judean, threw a pearl away
> Richer than all his tribe.

Instead of an Indian, we have a Jew. Instead of a struggle between Othello's conflicting national and racial identities, we have a struggle between religious identities. The line poignantly alludes to Othello's failure to live up to his adopted Christianity. Or rather, it would poignantly allude to Othello's failure to live up to his adopted Christianity, if *Judean* is the right word.

One of these interpretations must be wrong—the line has to be either about an Indian or a Judean—but it is impossible to tell which. The compositors, who set the type by hand into the presses for both the Quarto and the Folio, had to place the letters in upside down and backward; mistakes were common. It would be so easy to misread *Indian* as *Judean* or the other way around. Which line is Shakespeare's? You choose. Keep in mind that this is a single line from *Othello*. There are twelve extant versions of *Richard*

III. Pericles exists in just one single terrible quarto—we can only imagine what a decent edition would look like. Editing *Hamlet* is a good way to wreck your life.

There are two possible responses to this multiplicity of Shakespearean texts. The old-fashioned way is to assume that Shakespeare held an ideal play in his perfect mind when he wrote it, and that the job of the editor is to uncover that ideal play. In this model, the editor struggles with the discrepancies between the drafts, the depredations of the scatterbrained and scatterfingered compositors who set the text, and arrives at Shakespeare's original intentions. The British scholar Harold Jenkins—a genius editor if ever one existed—spent his time on earth doing just so, and presented the monumental Arden edition of *Hamlet* as the fruit. It remains the definitive conflation of the play. The new editorial strategy is to present readers with choices, two different *Hamlets*, one Folio, one Quarto. For the conflators, Shakespeare is a god, a unified creator of self-conscious masterpiece. For the separators, Shakespeare was more a man of the world, a producer, an actor, a man who worked in drafts and was not above chopping his stuff up to fit the necessities of touring.

Writers are not scholars or editors. They certainly

aren't bibliographers. Many great writers have typically taken little care with the printing of their works. John Keats produced three separate, equally valid, versions of "Ode on a Grecian Urn," each with significant differences. James Joyce made corrections on the proof copy of *Ulysses*, infuriating his editors. Marcel Proust was similarly careless with *Remembrance of Things Past*. Shakespeare was a sloppy god, which isn't that unusual in literature. Why would he care about the printing in the Second Quarto of *Hamlet*? He wasn't going to get paid whether it was good or bad, and besides he was in the middle of writing *Macbeth*.

Not that the carelessness of the master compensates his readers, who want to know what he wrote and, through his writing, who he was. We're left with a syllogism: To know Shakespeare we have to know the texts, but to know the texts we already have to have an idea of who Shakespeare was. Even more frustrating are the missing Shakespeare plays. How are we supposed to know what kind of artist he was when we don't have all his material? *Love's Labour's Won*, the sequel to *Love's Labour's Lost*, is mentioned in two different sources, one of which is a bookseller's list, which means that the play was most likely printed. And that means that, somewhere, in some attic, a printed copy of an entirely unknown play by Shakespeare is lying untouched and unread. (I get shivers just thinking about it.) Even more tantalizing is the possibility of *Cardenio*, which the editor Lewis Theobald discovered in manuscript form in 1727 and which was subsequently lost in a fire. Scholars assume from the title that the play was a Shakespearean adaptation of scenes from *Don Quixote*. Imagine: a fusion of Shakespeare and Cervantes, the original playwright and the original novelist. The history of European literature would have to be rewritten.

So we don't know the facts of his life, what he looked like, or what his work is supposed to look like, but I would say that there's an even deeper sense in which Shakespeare is unknowable. The work we have is unfathomable. There's always more. His depths are abyssal. It took me maybe fifty readings of *Hamlet* to notice the trick in the opening lines:

> *Francisco at his post. Enter to him Barnardo*
> BARNARDO: Who's there?
> FRANCISCO: Nay, answer me: stand, and unfold
>   yourself.
>
> (1.1.1–2)

See it? The order of the questioning is wrong. Barnardo, who arrives to relieve Francisco, is the one who is demanding proof of identity. Francisco should be asking and Barnardo should be answering. *Hamlet* begins with a mistake. This mistake occurs at the border of Elsinore castle, the political border, the border of Hamlet's family, the border of the self, where ghosts emerge to haunt their sons, the border between the living and the dead, between the material world and the world of the spirit, at the border of the play, in the space between the actors and the audience. The anxious machinery of the entirety of *Hamlet* is predicted by the first two words, and they are a mistaken "Who's there?"

"Who's there?" is exactly the question that never receives an answer from Shakespeare. And yet we can never stop asking it. The source of all this power, all these incredible effects spawned by his masterpieces, remains hidden, despite our best attempts at discovery. Sane, honest people have to be satisfied with a shadowy half absence, half presence—even scholars who enjoy speculating about who he might have been and under what impetus he composed his work. But of course at any given time, only a fraction of the world is sane *and* honest. The identity of Shakespeare has provoked more humbug than any other literary question, with the false searchers congregating into two great tribes, the frauds and the crazies.

The greatest of the frauds has to be William-Henry Ireland, who, during the late eighteenth century, committed perhaps the boldest forgeries of all time. His father, Samuel Ireland, owned a rather decent collection of antiquities, including a selection of Hogarths, and even a Rubens and a Van Dyck, along with several curiosities: a bit of cerecloth from a mummy, a portion of a cloak belonging to Charles I, that sort of thing. He coveted Shakespeareana most of all. Four times a week after dinner, Samuel would divide parts of a Shakespeare play among his family for public reading and discussion. By all accounts the father loved Shakespeare more than he loved his son.

William-Henry was dull, the perfect cover for a fraud. According to a headmaster's note that accompanied him home one year, he was "so stupid as to be a disgrace to the school." At the Shakespearean evenings, he would sit and listen mutely to the conversation without offering any opinion. One evening, in a fit of Shakespeare enthusiasm, Samuel declared himself willing to trade half his library for a single signature from the great man. Soon after, on December 2, 1794, William-Henry managed to surprise his father with a wonderful discovery. He had found a Shakespeare signature on a mortgage deed, cosigned by Shakespeare's business partner John Heminge. And where had William-Henry found the precious document? In the home of a mysterious Mr. H., who consented to allow William-Henry to take the original documents only after swearing an oath never to disclose the location of his house and after allowing sufficient time for the documents to be copied. The original's paper was from Shakespeare's time, appropriately aged, and the ink was typical of the period. Samuel believed it to be genuine but still brought it to the College of Arms for confirmation. They authenticated the document as well.

William-Henry soon began bringing other wonders from the house of Mr. H. In the large chest that the "gentleman of fortune" kept in his no doubt stately mansion, William-Henry came across a promissory note from Shakespeare to Heminge, for five pounds, five shillings. The find was tremendous, being the only promissory note surviving from Shakespeare's time.

Clearly Shakespeare had been a very honest man, scrupulous in his business dealings. Then William-Henry uncovered a letter from Shakespeare to Lord Southampton thanking him for his patronage, a beautifully felicitous solution to the problem that had consumed scholars for generations, of how Shakespeare had afforded his initial stake in the Lord Chamberlain's Company.

Mr. H.'s marvelous chest slowly began to yield up even more wonderful treasures. William-Henry, after a few weeks of searching, uncovered Shakespeare's profession of faith—the final proof of his commitment to Protestantism—which ended with the immortal line:

> Forgyve O Lorde alle oure Synnes ande withe thye greate goodnesse take usse alle to thye Breaste O cherishe usse like the sweete Chickenne thatte under the coverte offe herre spredynge Wings Receyves herre lyttle Broode ande hoveringe oerre themme keeps themme harmlesse ande in safetye.

The great scholar Dr. Warton, on hearing the profession read out loud, declared: "Sir, we have many very fine passages in our church service, and our Litany abounds with beauties; but here, sir, here is a man who has distanced us all!" Samuel could not have asked for more.

There were, William-Henry claimed, over eleven hundred books from Shakespeare's personal library in that mysterious house, many of which had been annotated by Shakespeare himself. He brought a love letter from Shakespeare to Anne Hathaway, which proved that he was just the decent family man Samuel always assumed him to be. The portrait which emerged of the Bard was what Samuel expected in all respects: a loving husband, decent citizen, fair businessman, close to the aristocracy, and in all respects a true English gentleman.

And then at last, with a great splurge, the true jewels. First, a copy of *Lear* in Shakespeare's handwriting, a final draft of one of his greatest plays with the veil of compositors torn back. *Lear* as Shakespeare wanted it to be. It would be hard to imagine a greater scholarly discovery. Then it came. A new play. A completely new play by Shakespeare. The plot taken from the English history of Holinshed. The title *Vortigern*. It took William-Henry over two weeks to bring the play to his father, because Mr. H. insisted on copies of everything before releasing manuscripts to the public, but how many scholars in history had been lucky enough to stumble on new Shakespeare material? Samuel immediately undertook negotiations with several important theater producers.

The existence of a new play raised the stakes on the Shakespeare discoveries. From the beginning, the public's response to the manuscripts had been mixed. A few journalists doubted the testimonials of authenticity, impugning Samuel's reputation, but support for the genuineness of the manuscripts came from the most eminent personalities of the age, including William Pitt the Younger; the philosopher Edmund Burke; Richard Sheridan, who agreed to produce the opening night of *Vortigern*; as well as countless members of the aristocracy. The great James Boswell, biographer of Samuel Johnson, knelt to kiss the manuscript in reverence and thanked God that he had lived to see the day of its discovery.

Doubt persisted. Several journalists wrote nasty parodies, poking fun at the Bard's strange spelling in the manuscripts. One wrote a fake letter from Shakespeare to Ben Jonson:

Tooo Missteerree Beenjaammiinnee Joohnnssonn

DEEREE SIRREE,

Wille youe doee meee theee favvourree too dinnee wytthee meee onnn Friddaye nextte attt twoo off theee clocke too eatee somme muttonne choppes andd somme pottaattooeessee

I amm deeerree sirree

Yourre goodde friendde

WILLIIAME SHAEKSPARE.

During all this drama, it never occurred to Samuel that his son could be a forger, even when incredible documents kept appearing right after they were mentioned at his after-dinner Shakespeare soirees. How could a dull boy like William-Henry, a cowardly boy, manufacture such a staggering collection? *Vortigern*, the play he had brought from Mr. H., was considered by leading experts of the day to be among Shakespeare's most finished plays. Consider lines like these:

> Give me a sword!
> I have so clogg'd and badged this with blood
> And slippery gore, that it doth mock my gripe.
> A sword! I say.

Could William-Henry, his twenty-year-old dolt of a son, have composed such immortalities?

The attacks by the press grew harsher and more confident the more material they were given to work with. William-Henry refused to give his father the access that he needed to prove their innocence—he had sworn a vow, he claimed. And then the Irelands had the misfortune to run into Edmond Malone, the most compulsively detail-oriented Shakespeare editor of all time. Malone took ninety pages of scholarship to obliterate the claim to authenticity of a single document in the Mr. H. manuscripts, a letter Queen Elizabeth supposedly wrote to Shakespeare. Ninety pages to describe the fraud contained in fifty words. There was just so much fraud to describe. The Queen's handwriting wasn't the same as in her genuine letters; she confused her own palace with the town next to it and misspelled basic words like *ande* and *forre* and *Londonne*. The name *Leycester* was written "Leicester," and he was incorrectly referred to as "his Grace." The manuscript used Arabic instead of Roman numerals. At the date it was supposedly written, it was impossible for Elizabeth to be where she said she was. The Queen mentions a cedar tree; there were no cedar trees in England at that time. The whole mess blew up before the opening night of the Sheridan-produced *Vortigern*. The audience laughed at the tragedy. The audience laughed at Shakespearean tragedy. William-Henry disappeared, and all the prestigious support evaporated. Samuel would have been justified in shouting, as Timon does to his false friends: "Live loath'd and long, most smiling, smooth detested parasites."

The aftermath of the fraud was a kind of perverted wish fulfillment for the Irelands. They got everything they wanted, backward. Samuel was immortalized onstage, just as he always wanted, but as the buffoonish Sir Bamber Blackletter in Frederick Reynolds's *Fortune's Fool*, a hit play at Covent Garden. William-Henry took encouragement from the fact that leading literary experts of his day easily believed that he was Shakespeare, and wrote sixty middling books over the course of a middling career. Like most hack writers, he hit lucky and unlucky patches. He spent time in debtors' prison but met Napoleon, which seems like a fair trade to me.

The crazies are worse than the frauds, and their lives tend to be even more grotesque. The frauds at least know that they themselves are frauds. The crazies believe that Shakespeare is the fraud. In the still air of his incomplete biography, they sniff out the delicious odor of conspiracy. How could Shakespeare have been the same man who didn't even know how to sign his own name? He must have been somebody else. Anti-Stratfordianism—the loose term for the various theories rejecting Shakespeare's traditional identity—is mostly a gentle madness, the literary equivalent of the flat-earth theory or séances. To put the matter in perspective: Not a single PhD dissertation has ever been accepted, by any university, from an anti-Stratfordian, just as no astronomy department grants PhDs to people who believe in the Ptolemaic system of heavenly spheres.

The original, and the greatest, of the anti-Stratfordians was a Boston woman named Delia Bacon. When she published her masterpiece, *The Philosophy of the Plays of*

Shakespere Unfolded, in 1857, a few authors before her had tentatively suggested that the man named Shakespeare was an elaborate cover for the play's true author. *Shakespere Unfolded* sparked the mass mania that continues into the present day. Delia Bacon, in addition to having complete self-confidence and single-mindedness of purpose unimpeded by worry about the facts—she did not bother to examine any manuscripts in the British Museum, for example—was also a writer of splendid intensity. *Shakespeare Unfolded* is unreadable. Not even its most devoted adherents claimed to have read the whole thing. But at times it can reach utter brilliance:

> It is not this old actor of Elizabeth's time, who exhibited these plays at his theatre in the way of his trade, and cared for them precisely as a tradesman would—cared for them as he would have cared for tin kettles, or earthen pans and pots, if they had been in his line, instead; it is not this old tradesman; it is not this old showman and hawker of plays; it is not this old lackey, whose hand is on all our heart-strings, whose name is, of mortal names, the most awe-inspiring.

The passage is the most eloquent expression of the fundamental premise of all anti-Stratfordian arguments: that Shakespeare was far too pedestrian a man to have composed the plays that bear his name.

Delia Bacon was a groupist; she believed that Shakespeare was the pen name for a group of the Elizabethan age's greatest minds, including Sir Walter Raleigh, Francis Bacon, and Edmund Spenser. There are many different theories. Over fifty names have been put forward as the plays' true author, all richer and with more education than the real Shakespeare. The anti-Stratfordians are universally snobs. And worse, they're ignorant. The middle classes have produced almost all the greatest literature of England. John Keats spoke in a cockney accent. Charles Dickens worked at blacking bottles as a child. If Shakespeare were an aristocrat, he would have been an anomaly.

Nonetheless, Delia Bacon, like William-Henry Ireland, managed to convince some of the greatest men of her age to support her mad dream of establishing once and for all that Shakespeare wasn't Shakespeare. Ralph Waldo Emerson agreed with her. Nathaniel Hawthorne wrote a letter of introduction to Thomas Carlyle when she traveled to London. She made favorable impressions on all of these great men. Unfortunately, despite her evident brilliance, her mental health problems began to overwhelm her once she arrived in England. In search of proof, she snuck one night onto Bacon's grave, inside which she was convinced the great man had left a cipher that connected the various parts of her theory together. With the shovel in hand, she lost faith, panicked, and ran away. After that incident, she spent most of the rest of her life in an asylum, dying two years after the publication of her book, alone and in a foreign land, deserving a better cause and a more decent fate.

The interest in the Bacon theory did not die with Delia Bacon. It died when several strong scholarly biographies of Francis Bacon appeared and made it impossible, even to the insane, for him to be the author of Shakespeare's plays. In 1920, the Bacon theory was replaced by the Oxford theory, which states that Edward de Vere, Seventeenth Earl of Oxford, wrote Shakespeare's plays. The aptly named John Looney, who was rejected by one publisher because he wouldn't adopt a pseudonym, first proposed the theory in his *"Shakespeare" Identified* in 1920. Looney was self-consciously an amateur. The reason the mystery of Shakespeare's identity had not been solved, he claimed in the introduction of his book, was that "it has been left mainly in the hands of literary men."

Looney's method was simple. Proceeding from the assumption that the author of Shakespeare's plays had to be a great man, he looked around for a great man. He selected the aspects of Shakespeare's personality that such a genius must exhibit—"apparently eccentric and mysterious," "not adequately appreciated," "an enthusiast in the world of drama," and "a lyric poet of recognized talent," among others—and eventually hit on Edward de Vere. John Aubrey in his *Brief Lives* has a great story about Edward de Vere, which Looney never mentions: "This Earl of Oxford, making of his low obeisance to Queen Elizabeth, happened to let a fart, at which he was so ashamed that he went to travel, 7 years." When he returned to court after his travels, the Queen declared on seeing him again, "My Lord, I had forgot the fart." Recent biographical work has uncovered that the Seventeenth Earl of Oxford was a pedophile and murderer as well as a flatulator. If de Vere were the author of Shakespeare's plays, we would have to explain how such a nasty bit of business could write such masterpieces.

It is to the great disgrace of journalism that the Oxfordian thesis is occasionally mooted as a genuine competitor with the "theory" that Shakespeare was Shakespeare. Of course great men have supported and continue to support Looney's idea, as great men supported the Irelands and Delia Bacon. Sigmund Freud (an Oedipal murder of his intellectual father?) and the well-respected United States Supreme Court Justice John Paul Stevens are both believers. The problems with the Oxfordian thesis are glaring and obvious. The hidden identity would, first of all, involve a giant conspiracy inveigling not only Shakespeare's fellow writers such as Ben Jonson, who refers to Shakespeare as a living friend, but also countless diaries and legal documents relating to the theater. It would also assume that such a conspiracy could be completely concealed from archivists and scholars for four centuries. Also, Edward de Vere died in 1604. How he managed to write plays that fit the topicalities of the moment a decade after his death is difficult to fathom. To refer to political activities that occurred postmortem is truly a magnificent feat of writerly skill. A few basic facts also elude Looney and the Oxfordians. Edward de Vere did not know Latin. Shakespeare's plays were written by somebody who did.

Edward de Vere knew nothing about the countryside of Warwickshire, or leatherworking, or the intricacies of stagecraft, whereas the author of Shakespeare's plays knew all of these worlds intimately.

Let me repeat, for any of you doubters out there. Edward de Vere died in 1604. Shakespeare wrote until 1616.

I know that I will convince nobody by this simple recitation of the obvious, because conspiracy theorists find confirmation in the facts that refute their claims. The nutjobs will find the patterns everywhere, in everything. The Shakespeare codes that lunatic researchers have "uncovered" are so varied and so numerous that it's hard to pick the craziest. They are at least as fun as cryptic crosswords. Take the case of the "long word" from *Love's Labour's Lost*. A clown remarks, "I marvell thy M. hath not eaten thee for a word, for thou art not so long by the head as honorificabilitudinitatibus: Thou are easier swallowed then a flapdragon." The same word, splayed out in an elaborate diagram, can be found in Bacon's papers in the British Museum. From this coincidence much weighty conclusion has been drawn. In 1897 Dr. Isaac Platt believed he had found the hidden code contained in the word. First he broke it into two pieces, which gives, reading the first part backwards: 1) BACIFIRONOH and 2) ILITUDINITATIBUS. The first he took to be the signature FR BACONO, and the second LUDI TUITI NATI, the leftover letters spelling HI SIBI. Which together makes up HI LUDI, TUITI SIBI, FR. BACONO NATI, or "These plays, produced by Francis Bacon, guarded for themselves." The great American cryptologists William and Elizabeth Friedman, wartime codebreakers who turned their attention to Shakespeare ciphers as a hobby, remarked, "There must be an easier way of leaving one's name for posterity."

But folly about Shakespeare can only ever be comparative. Everyone manufactures their own Shakespeare. Some find ciphers in random weird long words. Some buy obviously fake portraits. Others sift the residue of his plays in the quest for his ideal versions. Yet others troll the antiquaries in the hope of a promissory note or a bill of sale bearing his signature. The whole world is Shakespeare-crazy. His vision of life has been propelled across the earth through the eyes and mouths of sailors, cowboys, assassins, sexual revolutionists, Nazis, Communists, freedom riders, and genteel introducers of birds to foreign continents. Shakespeare has quite by accident conjured up a froth of consequence. The world teems with him.

Shakespeare himself is nowhere to be found in all these teeming effects. He stands apart. He is alone. Shakespeare may reflect the dazzling beauty of the world and everything in it, of men corrupted by ambition and lust, wives triumphant and defeated, love of all shapes and all kinds and all degrees of force, death by surprise or by expectation, funny drunks, sexy middle-aged women, lovely falling leaves, guilty bloodstains, but he himself is swallowed in the reflection, a dark origin to a vast illumination. His art was to reflect the world as accurately and as fully as possible, and he achieved his goal by becoming as beautiful and surprising and mysterious and unfathomable as the world itself.

The great short-story writer Jorge Luis Borges offered an alternative fictionalized biography of Shakespeare in his parable "Everything and Nothing." Shakespeare, for Borges, is haunted by his own absence. He is "only a bit of coldness, a dream dreamt by no one" who has to pretend to be other people because he is no one himself. From that missing personality, an identity gone missing, he conjures the varied characters of his work. The story ends with Shakespeare confronting God:

> History adds that before or after dying he found himself in the presence of God and told Him: "I who have been so many men in vain want to be one and myself." The voice of the Lord answered from a whirlwind: "Neither am I anyone; I have dreamt the world as you dreamt your work, my Shakespeare, and among the forms in my dream are you, who like myself are many and no one."

Who's there? The player king in *Hamlet*'s play-within-a-play offers a kind of answer:

> Our thoughts are ours. Their ends none of our own.

ACKNOWLEDGMENTS

I am wildly grateful to my editor at HarperCollins, Julia Cheiffetz, whose counsel was invaluable, as was the hard work and persistence of Katie Salisbury. My agent, PJ Mark, was, as usual, tireless. Several magnificent readers—Stephen Brooke, Julian Porter, Robert Fulford, and Alexander Leggatt—polished my best stuff and rooted out the embarrassments from early drafts, for which I am deeply grateful. A generous grant from the Toronto Arts Council helped enormously during the writing of this book.

NOTES

INTRODUCTION: ALL THE WORLD'S A STAGE

The details of the Carriacou Mas came from Joan Fayer and Joan McMurray's "The Carriacou Mas as 'Syncretic Artifact,'" *Journal of American Folklore* 112, no. 443 (Winter 1999), pp. 58–73; and Craig Dionne's "Commonplace Literacy and the Colonial Scene: The Case of Carriacou's Shakespeare Mas," from *Native Shakespeares: Indigenous Appropriations on a Global Stage* (Bodmin, Cornwall, UK: MPG Books, 2008).

THE FORTUNES OF THE MOOR

The details of Paul Robeson's life came almost entirely from Martin Duberman's *Paul Robeson: A Biography*

(New York: New Press, 1988), although a few details appeared in Paul Robeson Jr.'s *The Undiscovered Paul Robeson: an Artist's Journey 1889–1939* (New York: John Wiley & Sons, 2001). The sketchier, more difficult life story of Ira Aldridge came from the essays collected in *Ira Aldridge: The African Roscius*, ed. Bernth Lindfors (Rochester, NY: University of Rochester Press, 2007). I was also helped by Jyotsna Singh's "Othello's Identity, Postcolonial Theory, and Contemporary African Rewritings of *Othello*," in *Othello*, ed. Lena Cowen Orlin (New York: Palgrave Macmillan, 2004); Michael Neill's "Unproper Beds: Race, Adultery, and the Hideous in *Othello*," *Shakespeare Quarterly* 40, no. 4 (Winter 1989), pp. 383–412; Coppélia Kahn's "Forbidden Mixtures: Shakespeare in Blackface Minstrelsy, 1844," in *Shakespeare and the Cultures of Performance*, ed. Paul Yachnin and Patricia Badir (London: Ashgate, 2008) pp. 121–44; and Tilden Edelstein's "*Othello* in America: The Drama of Racial Intermarriage," *Region, Race and Reconstruction: Essays in Honor of C. Vann Woodward*, ed. Morgan Kousser and James McPherson (Oxford: Oxford University Press, 1982).

WORDS, WORDS, WORDS

The most useful reference texts on Shakespeare's language are David Crystal's *Think on My Words*: *Exploring Shakespeare's Language* (Cambridge, UK: Cambridge University Press, 2008); and Jeffrey McQuain and Stanley Malless's *Coined by Shakespeare*: *Words and Meanings First Penned by the Bard* (New York: Merriam-Webster, 1997). Richard Schoch's *Not Shakespeare*: *Burlesque and Bardolatry in the Nineteenth Century* (Cambridge, UK: Cambridge University Press, 2002) was the source for the material on burlesques. The Bernard Levin passage comes from his collection *Enthusiasms* (London: Jonathan Cape, 1983). Sandy Leggatt suggested to me in conversation that Caliban may himself have generated *scamel* as a word from his own private language.

THE BEAST WITH TWO BACKS

The details of the dirty stuff came from two wonderful books: Eric Partridge's *Shakespeare's Bawdy* (London: Routledge & Kegan Paul, 1947) and Pauline Kiernan's *Filthy Shakespeare*: *Shakespeare's Most Outrageous Puns* (London: Quercus, 2006). Kenneth Tynan's experience with *Titus* can be found in *The Methuen Book of Shakespeare Anecdotes* (London: Methuen Drama, 1992). Thomas Bowdler's history is well documented in several different places: Noel Perrin's *Doctor Bowdler's Legacy*: *A History of Expurgated Books in England and America* (Boston: Godine, 1969); Marvin Rosenberg's "Reputation, Oft Lost Without Deserving . . . ," *Shakespeare Quarterly* 9, no. 4 (Autumn 1958), pp. 499–506; Michael Dobson's "Bowdler and Britannia: Shakespeare and the National Libido," in *Shakespeare and Race*, ed. Catherine Alexander (Cambridge, UK: Cambridge University Press, 2000) pp. 112–23; and Donald Hedrick's "Flower Power: Shakespearean Deep Bawdy and the Botanical Perverse," *The Administration of Aesthetics*: *Censorship, Political Criticism, and the Public Sphere* (Minneapolis: University of Minnesota Press, 1994). Research into Shakespeare's influence on Freud came from Julia Reinhard Lupton and Kenneth Reinhard's *After Oedipus*: *Shakespeare in Psychoanalysis* (Ithaca, NY: Cornell University Press, 1993); and Philip Armstrong's *Shakespeare in Psychoanalysis* (London: Routledge, 2001).

FLAMING YOUTH

Obviously, Philippe Ariès's masterpiece *Centuries of Childhood*: *A Social History of Family Life*, trans. Robert Baldick

(New York: Vintage Books, 1962) was essential. There are several excellent essays on Shakespeare's use in pop culture in *Shakespeare and Youth Culture*, ed. Jennifer Hulbert, Kevin Wetmore, and Robert York (New York: Palgrave Connect, 2006); and *Shakespeare After Mass Media*, ed. Richard Burt (New York: Palgrave Macmillan, 2002). Particularly good was Stephen Buhler's "Reviving Juliet, Repackaging Romeo: Transformations of Character in Pop and Post-Pop Music" from the latter book. The material on Ophelia came from Kimberly Rhodes's *Ophelia and Victorian Visual Culture: Representing Body Politics in the Nineteenth Century* (London: Ashgate, 2008); and Carol Solomon Kiefer's *The Myth and Madness of Ophelia* (Amherst, MA: Mead Art Museum, 2001). The performance history of *Romeo and Juliet* comes from Jill Levenson's introduction to the Oxford edition of the play and Katherine Wright's *Shakespeare's "Romeo and Juliet" in Performance: Traditions and Departures* (Lewiston, NY: Mellen University Press, 1997).

ALL HONORABLE MEN

Albert Furtwangler's *Assassin on Stage: Brutus, Hamlet and the Death of Lincoln* (Urbana: University of Illinois Press, 1991) is a superb study of the night Lincoln was killed and the various nights leading up to it. Alison Plowden's *The Elizabethan Secret Service* (London: Palgrave Macmillan, 1991); David Daniell's introduction to the Arden edition of *Julius Caesar*; and Robert Miola's "*Julius Caesar* and the Tyrannicide Debate," *Renaissance Quarterly* 38, no. 2 (Summer 1985) pp. 271–89 were also of great use.

TO HOLD THE MIRROR UP TO NATURE

The details about the history and biology of starlings came principally from Christopher Feare's *The Starling* (Oxford: Oxford University Press, 1984); and a chapter in Kim Todd's *Tinkering with Eden*: *A Natural History of Exotic Species in America* (New York: Norton & Norton, 2001). Also of use were Charles Elton's *The Ecology of Invasions of Animals and Plants* (Chicago: University of Chicago Press, 2000); and Ted Gup's article "100 Years of the Starling," from the *New York Times*, September 1, 1990.

GIVE ME MY ROBE, PUT ON MY CROWN

The details about Shakespeare, Communism, and Czechoslovakian theater come from Zdenek Stribrny's *The Whirligig of Time*: *Essays on Shakespeare and Czechoslovakia*, ed.

Lois Potter (Cranbury, NJ: Rosemont, 2001). The reception history of *The Merchant of Venice* comes from Rodney Symington's *The Nazi Appropriation of Shakespeare*: *Cultural Politics in the Third Reich* (New York: Edwin Mellen Press, 2005); as well as Sabine Schülting's "'I Am Not Bound to Please Thee with My Answers': *The Merchant of Venice* on the Post-war German Stage," in *World-wide Shakespeares*: *Local Appropriations in Film and Performance*, ed. Sonia Massai (New York: Routledge, 2005); and Avraham Oz's "Transformations of Authenticity: *The Merchant of Venice* in Israel," in *Foreign Shakespeare*: *Contemporary Performance*, ed. Dennis Kennedy (Cambridge, UK: Cambridge University Press, 1993). Marjorie Garber's *Shakespeare and Modern Culture* (New York: Anchor, 2009) and *Profiling Shakespeare* (New York: Routledge, 2008) were useful to me both in this essay and in several others.

NOT MARBLE, NOR THE GILDED MONUMENTS

The details about the Gold Rush come from a magnificent short study by Helene Wickham Koon, *How Shakespeare Won the West*: *Players and Performances in America's Gold Rush, 1849–1865* (New York: Macfarland, 1989). *Tolstoy on Shakespeare* has, to my knowledge, never been reprinted. The American edition from 1903, which I used, contained the juicy letter from Shaw that I have quoted, as well as the collection of anti-Shakespeare notices from the press. George Orwell's essay "Lear, Tolstoy and the Fool," published in the journal *Polemic* 7, March 1947, appears in the collection *All Art Is Propaganda*, ed. George Packer (London: First Mariner Books, 2009). Wilson-Knight's *Shakespeare and Tolstoy* (Oxford: Oxford University Press, 1934) and George Gibian's *Tolstoj and Shakespeare* (Gravenhage: Mouton, 1957) were useful. The details of Chekhov's life come from Daniel Gillès's 1967 biography *Chekhov: Observer Without Illusion*, trans. Charles Lam Markmann (New York: Funk & Wagnalls, 1968).

A KING OF INFINITE SPACE

Laura Bohannan told her story of storytelling with the Tiv in "Shakespeare in the Bush," *Natural History*, August–September 1966.

TO BE OR NOT TO BE

The biographical information on Shakespeare, as well as the descriptions of the legends surrounding him, came principally from two books by Samuel Schoenbaum, *Shakespeare's Lives* (Oxford: Clarendon Press, 1970) and *William Shakespeare: A Compact Documentary Life*, rev. ed. (Oxford: Oxford University Press, 1987). Stephanie Nolen's *Shakespeare's Face* (Toronto: Knopf, 2002) provided a useful survey of the debates around Shakespeare's portraiture. Also, Ron Rosenbaum's *The Shakespeare Wars: Clashing Scholars, Public Fiascoes, Palace Coups* (New York: Random House, 2006) was incredibly good, particularly about the debates around editorial practices. William and Elizabeth Friedman's *The Shakespeare Ciphers Examined: An Analysis of Cryptographic Systems Used as Evidence That an Author Other Than William Shakespeare Wrote the Plays Commonly Attributed to Him* (Cambridge, UK: Cambridge University Press, 1987) had all the details about the codes in Shakespeare anyone might want or need.

About the Author

Stephen Marche is a novelist who writes a monthly column for *Esquire* magazine about culture. Ten years ago, he chose Shakespeare as the subject of his PhD because, he believed, Shakespeare would never bore him. He was correct. The best job he ever had was as a professor of Renaissance drama at The City College of New York, which he quit in 2007 to write full-time. He lives in Toronto, Canada. Visit his website at www.StephenMarche.com